Something to Read 2

A reader for lower-intermediate students of English

Christine Lindop and Dominic Fisher

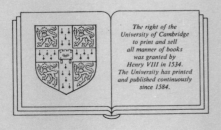

The right of the
University of Cambridge
to print and sell
all manner of books
was granted by
Henry VIII in 1534.
The University has printed
and published continuously
since 1584.

Cambridge University Press
Cambridge
New York   Port Chester
Melbourne   Sydney

Published by the Press Syndicate of the University of Cambridge
The Pitt Building, Trumpington Street, Cambridge CB2 1RP
40 West 20th Street, New York, NY 10011, USA
10 Stamford Road, Oakleigh, Melbourne 3166, Australia

© Cambridge University Press 1989

First published 1989

Printed in Great Britain
by Scotprint Ltd, Musselburgh, Scotland

ISBN 0 521 35686 5

Contents

Introduction

To the reader

Welcome to *Something to Read 2*, a collection of 32 short texts on a variety of subjects for Elementary and Lower-Intermediate students of English. As you'll see from the *Contents* page, there are three groups of texts; the first group is easier than the second, and the second is easier than the third. In each group, also, the early texts are usually simpler than the later ones. You don't have to start reading at the beginning of the book; you can simply look for topics that interest you personally. Then, we hope, you'll be *reading*, and not just practising your English.

We believe that it's useful for you to include in your reading the sort of English that you'll meet in real life. Many texts therefore include extracts from books, magazines etc. Sometimes, where you see [...], we've made a long or difficult extract shorter.

When you're reading, we suggest that you concentrate on general meaning first rather than trying to understand every word. In other words, try not to use a dictionary all the time. Where we feel that a dictionary would be particularly helpful, we tell you. Some texts include an activity marked ★. The activities are intended to give you help with meaning and an opportunity to check your reading, if you want it. They are not tests of memory, so do look at the text while you're doing them. The answers are on pages 58–59.

We hope you enjoy the book!

To the teacher

Something to Read 2 is intended to provide more extensive reading practice than is generally possible in a course book. With this book the choice of what, when and how much to read is, we feel, best left to the students. The teacher's role, as we see it, is to make the book available, although you might like to provide time in class for students to talk about what they've read. To start your students off, we suggest that you simply encourage them to choose a text and start reading, though you may also like to go through the introduction with them and make sure they understand it.

The level of this book is about the same as Level 2 of the Cambridge English Course.

Beginnings

Firsts

- The first roller skates were made in 1760 by Joseph Merlin, a Belgian musician. People at a dance couldn't believe it when Merlin arrived on his roller skates playing the violin. Unfortunately his skates had no brakes so he couldn't stop; he went straight across the dance floor and crashed into a large mirror. Both the mirror and the violin were broken, and Merlin was badly hurt. It was the last time anyone tried roller-skating for another hundred years.
- The first crossword puzzle was published in 1913.

- Strawberries also first came from the Americas. The kinds we eat now were first produced in the eighteenth century in France from a hybrid of *Fragaria virginiana* – a North American strawberry – and *Fragaria chiloensis*, a strawberry from Chile.

- Football's World Cup was started in Montevideo, Uruguay, by the Fédération Internationale de Football Association (FIFA) on 13 July 1930.
- The first ship to use the emergency signal SOS was the Titanic.

Bibles, babies and Aceeeffghhiillnnmmoorrssstuv

When did the world begin? Archbishop James Ussher (1581–1656) of Armagh, Northern Ireland, studied the Bible carefully and then said that the world began at 10 a.m. on 26 October, 4004 BC. Modern scientists, however, think it began 4,500 million years ago, and they don't give a time or date.

It's a long time before babies begin doing things for themselves. Some doctors think that this is because babies are born too soon. If they were born a few months later they could – like many baby animals – do more things without help. The reason this doesn't happen, of course, is that a baby would then be too big to leave the mother's body.

Lots of people begin life with a name that they

later change, but not many people do what Christoffel von Grimmelhausen did. This seventeenth century German writer took the letters of his name and made a new one – Aceeeffghhiillnnmmoorrssstuv.

⫸→

The beginning of a language

In 1880 thousands of immigrants arrived in Hawaii to work in the sugar industry. They came mainly from Japan, Korea, China, Spain and Portugal. Immediately there were big problems with language; the different groups couldn't understand one another, nor their employers (most of whom spoke English), nor the Hawaiian people.

By 1910, however, the immigrants were speaking a new language – Hawaiian Creole. It included words from all the original languages, but its grammar wasn't like any of them. Where had Hawaiian Creole come from? The immigrants, said Professor Derek Bickerton of the University of Hawaii, were too busy working to meet and talk to people from other language groups. He concluded that Hawaiian Creole must have been invented by the immigrants' children playing together, and that the parents had learnt the new language from their children.

Irma gets angry

★ Read this with a dictionary, but look up only the <u>underlined</u> words.

Husband has to clean house . . . by law!

by DENNIS NEWSON

A FED-UP wife has gone to law to get her <u>lazy</u> husband and idle son to do the housework – and she's won.

Irma Gross got a <u>lawyer</u> to draw up a <u>contract,</u> then warned the pair: "<u>Sign</u> it – or I walk out."

Hubby Conrad and son Herbert caved in*, and now they're running the family home in Bielefeld, West Germany.

Conrad, 56, who is retired, does the washing on Mondays, the shopping on Tuesdays and cooks and cleans the house on Thursdays and Fridays.

Herbert, 28, must dig the garden and clean the car.

Dirty

And if the pair fall down on the job* father must pay for a char* and son has to leave home.

Irma, 52, staged her <u>revolt</u> because she looked after the house AND went out to work part-time – but always came home to unmade beds and dirty dishes.

How are the two men coping? Conrad can't work the washing machine – and Herbert can't start the <u>lawn-mower</u>.

(from the *Daily Mirror*)

* *cave in:* finally agree to do something
* *fall down on the job:* don't do their work well
* *char:* person paid (usually by the hour) to clean houses

275 million years and still disgusting

'DIRTY', 'disgusting', 'horrible' – these are the sort of words that you probably think of when you see cockroaches. They are not very nice, but they are very successful.

They are much older than human beings: the earliest cockroaches lived about 275 million years ago, and they've hardly changed since then. They are international travellers; they've travelled by ship for hundreds of years, and more recently they've been found on planes too. They are also very good at making lots more cockroaches.

When a supermarket in East Osaka, Japan, offered a bounty* for each cockroach caught, it was inundated with 98,499 within a week. Two women collected 1,351 in just one apartment house.

Cockroaches can live almost anywhere. Luckily for us, only a few of the three to four thousand species of cockroach choose to share our buildings. If they decide to stay, however, it's very difficult to get rid of them. But then, the cockroach is not an ordinary insect.

*bounty: some money

[. . .] they can live for up to seven days after having their heads cut off [. . .]. Even more curious, they learn faster without their heads than with them.

It won't surprise you to learn that cockroaches aren't good to eat, but at least one person has tried. That person was Dr Frank Buckland, an English naturalist living in the last century. Known as 'the man who could eat anything', Buckland ate and enjoyed things like elephant, penguin and kangaroo – but cockroaches, he said, tasted horrible.

So what are cockroaches for? They seem to do only two things – eat, and produce more cockroaches – though they do both of them very well. It's possible that cockroaches help us – as some birds do – by eating rubbish. Like Dr Buckland, they seem to eat almost anything.

The cockroach [. . .] has been known to eat 'cooked potatoes, vegetables, flour pudding, dough and the like, dead and sick members of its own species, chocolate, honey, butter, vaseline, bread, flour, sugar, leather, wool items, rayon, shoe polish, book bindings, fruit and other items according to season.'

(from *Animal Oddities* by John May and Michael Marten)

Living in space

AS YOU probably know, the first person in space was the Russian astronaut Yuri Gagarin; he went into space for one hour and 48 minutes on 12 April 1961. Since then astronauts have stayed in space for longer periods, and both the Russians and the Americans now have plans for space stations where people can live and work comfortably for a very long time. So perhaps you'll be living in space one day; find out how much you know about it with this quiz.

★ The quiz will be easier to understand if you know the following words. Check their meanings in a dictionary before you begin.

blood   centrifuge   exercise
fire   gas   go out
gravity   meteorite   plant   strap

1. People first lived in space for more than three weeks:
    a) in the 1960s.
    b) in the 1970s.
    c) in the 1980s.

2. People travelling in space often feel ill for the same reason that people travelling by boat do. True or false?

3. Which of these are true? In space:
    a) you get shorter.
    b) your feet get smaller.
    c) you need less exercise.
    d) you look younger.

4. Astronauts are strapped into their beds so that they don't hurt themselves. True or false?

5. A fire on a spaceship goes out:
    a) faster than on earth.
    b) at the same speed as on earth.
    c) more slowly than on earth.

6. You can't grow plants in space because plants need gravity. True or false?

7. You're more likely to be hit by a large meteorite in a spaceship than in your house on earth. True or false?

8. Which of these are true? In space:
    a) men don't shave.
    b) you have to eat and drink from things like toothpaste tubes.
    c) toilets and showers are not very different from those on earth.

Answers

1. (b) in the 1970s. In 1971 Georgi Dobrovolski and Vladimir Volkov lived for 23 days in the Russian space station Salyut-1. Tragically, they died when they were coming back to earth. In 1973 Charles Conrad, Joseph Kerwin and Paul Weitz lived for 28 days in the American space station Skylab. Between 1973 and 1974 American astronauts stayed again on Skylab for 56 days and 84 days. By the 1980s living in space for even longer periods became possible, and Salyut-7 was lived in, by different astronauts, for 34 months.

American and Russian space ships Apollo and Soyuz meeting 140 miles above the earth

2. True. Both in a boat and in space it's often difficult to know what is 'up' and what is 'down'; this can make you feel ill.

3. (b) and (d) are true. Because there is no gravity in space more blood goes to the upper part of your body. This makes your feet a little smaller and your face fatter. Because your face is fatter there are fewer lines in it and you look younger. Your spine gets one or two inches longer too, and you need *more* exercise than on earth – because without gravity moving is easier.

4. True. An astronaut's sleeping bag is attached to the bed with straps. If this isn't done, the sleeping astronaut begins to move around the spaceship, pushed along by his or her own breath, and can easily hit something.

5. (a) faster than on earth. Because there is no gravity in a spaceship hot gases from a fire cannot rise; the gases stay near the fire, oxygen can't get to it and it soon goes out.

6. False. Most plants do need gravity but they can be grown in space inside a centrifuge. Centrifugal force gives the plants the 'gravity' they need.

7. False. You are just as likely to be hit by a large meteorite in your own house as in a spaceship.

8. Only (c) is true. Men can shave, if they want to, with a safety razor and shaving cream. In the past astronauts did eat and drink from tubes but now food and drink in space are very like food and drink on earth. A space toilet uses air not water but otherwise is similar to a toilet on earth. The only difference in a space shower is that your feet have to be strapped to the floor – and you *must* remember to shut the door. A bath, incidentally, is impossible.

5

Shadow pictures

IN EIGHTEENTH and nineteenth century Europe silhouettes were a cheap and popular way of making portraits. Nowadays when we want pictures of our families and friends we usually take photographs, but silhouettes can make an interesting change, and they are easy to do.

A silhouette is really just a copy of someone's shadow. This can be drawn on white paper and then filled in with black paint, or it can be drawn on black paper, cut out and stuck onto white or coloured paper. Here's how to make a silhouette of a head.

A nineteenth-century silhouette from the Victoria and Albert museum, London

How to make a silhouette

You will need:

sheet of paper
drawing pins or Blu Tack, to attach paper
   to wall
pencil
scissors
an unshaded electric light
black paper or paint

How to work

Sit your subject on a chair in a darkened room as close to the wall as possible, with profile parallel to the wall.

Pin a sheet of paper behind the sitter. Place a light in front of the sitter, so that the shadow of the face falls sharply on the paper.

Trace the outline of the profile on the paper.

If you work on black paper, life-size, the profile can now be cut out and mounted just as it is. If it is on white paper, you can cut it out and trace it on to black paper, or colour it.

(from *Crafts* by Valerie Jackson)

Tracing the profile

Making smaller portraits

The instructions on page 6 are for a life-size portrait, but you may want to make a smaller picture. Some art and photographic shops sell machines to help you do this, but it's probably easier (and cheaper) to use a photocopier.

1. First trace the outline of the profile on white paper, as above.
2. Use the photocopier to make a smaller copy of the outline.

3. Fill in the outline on the photocopy.
4. Mount and then frame the photocopy.

In fact, you could make a life-size silhouette exactly as Valerie Jackson says and *then* photocopy it. The only problem with this is that photocopiers don't always copy large areas of black very well.

Some other ideas

- You don't have to use black when you fill in the outline of your silhouette (though dark colours are best). Try dark brown, green or blue.

- Cut out your silhouette and stick it on coloured or gold paper before putting it in a frame.

- Cut a hole in a piece of dark paper, and put the paper on top of the silhouette before it goes into the frame.

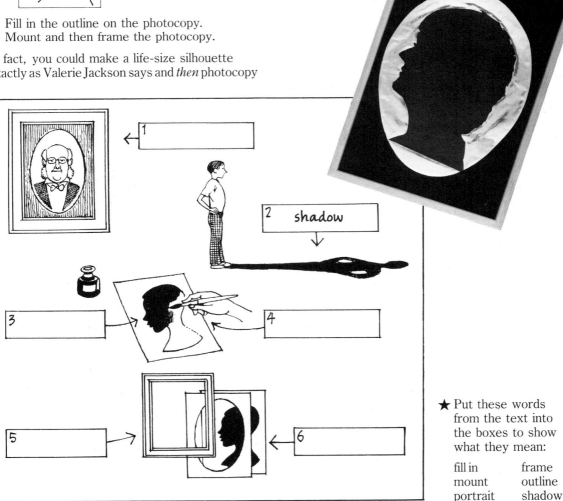

2 shadow

★ Put these words from the text into the boxes to show what they mean:

fill in   frame
mount   outline
portrait   shadow

Scallops

PILGRIM SCALLOP
Pecten jacobaeus (Linnaeus)

Remarks: The shells, which run up to 14cm, are often used as dishes for small servings of fish gratiné.

The scallops swim around by opening and closing their shells so that the expulsion of the water drives them along. The muscle joining the two halves of the shell is therefore large and powerful.

(from *Mediterranean Seafood* by Alan Davidson)

Perhaps you know the scallop as a tasty seafood, served in its own white shell. But the dinner table isn't the only place where you'll find it.

In the art gallery

Both the Roman goddess Venus and the Greek goddess Aphrodite were strongly associated with the sea. One story about Aphrodite said that she was born from a scallop shell, and there were Greek pictures showing Aphrodite rising from a scallop shell two thousand years before Botticelli painted his picture. Botticelli was simply using a very old idea in a new painting.

The Birth of Venus by Sandro Botticelli, 1478

On the road to Santiago de Compostela

Between the ninth and sixteenth centuries millions of people travelled from France, England, Germany and Italy to visit the tomb of St James at Santiago de Compostela in north-west Spain. This part of Spain was (and still is) famous for its shellfish. When the pilgrims arrived, they used to go and find a scallop shell on the beach, or buy one outside the cathedral, and take it home to show they had been to Santiago.

Later, travellers began to wear a scallop shell on their hats to show they were going to Santiago. Churches and other buildings along the road also showed the scallop shell, and some still do today.

St James with the scallop shell – a statue from the church of Santa Maria de Terra, Spain and the Cathedral church of Santiago de Compostela

On coats of arms

Scallop shells were quite often used like this. On very old coats of arms it sometimes meant that someone from that family had travelled as a pilgrim to Santiago de Compostela. A second reason was that the shell would remind people of your name, so families with surnames like Shelley used scallops in their coats of arms. A third reason was simply that people liked it; the shape of the scallop is easy to recognise and remember.

The coat of arms of the Shelley family

At petrol stations

In countries all over the world people recognise the white shell design that the Shell Company uses for its products, but the reason a shell was chosen has nothing to do with petrol.

[In 1897] Marcus Samuel Junior formed The Shell Transport and Trading Company to carry on the business of transporting and trading oil products, initially to the Far East. The name 'Shell' was chosen for the sentimental reason that Marcus Samuel Senior had started the family's Far East trade fifty or more years earlier by importing decorative oriental sea shells.

(from Shell Education Service material)

At first Shell used a mussel shell, but very soon they began to use a scallop instead. Over the years the design of the shell has changed, but you can still see that it's a scallop.

★ Choose the correct dates from the list and put them in the spaces (be careful: there are more dates than spaces).

the 1840s   1897   1900   1904   the 1940s   1971   1989

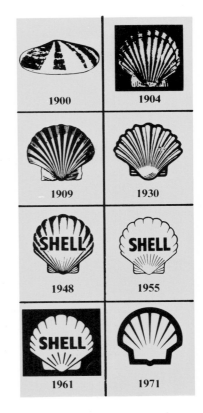

1900	1904
1909	1930
1948	1955
1961	1971

1897 ..... Marcus Samuel Junior started the Shell Transport and Trading Company.

..... The present Shell design was first used.

..... Marcus Samuel Senior started the family business buying shells in the Far East.

..... Shell used a scallop shell design for their products for the first time.

..... A mussel shell design was used for Shell products.

In buildings, furniture – and in the kitchen

The scallop has been a popular shape for more than 2,000 years. The flat shell fits nicely into a half-circle space, for example over a door or a window; the round shell fits well into a hemispherical space. From Greek and Roman times to the present you can find the shape of the scallop in ceilings and walls, in basins and bowls, and even in spoons. Perhaps it's not surprising that the shell itself is still used as a bowl for seafood and fish.

The sky is still blue

IMAGINE going blind. Imagine not being able to see your children, your wife or husband or your friends. Think of the ordinary things you couldn't do, such as reading a book or looking at the sky. Now imagine being partially blind; you can see enough to look after your children, but not enough to see them smile or to read them a story. Then think how you would feel – after many years of blindness – going into hospital for an operation that might restore your sight. Very likely you would be afraid of still being blind after the operation – but at the same time hoping very much that you would soon be able to open your eyes and actually see. Brian Mason and Angela Waters, living on opposite sides of the world, were in that situation.

Angela is a 25-year-old mother of four children from Scunthorpe, South Humberside, in England. At the age of 17 she got an eye disease; she became totally blind in one eye and could see very little with the other. Thanks to a recent operation – and thanks to an older woman, Mary Bedford – she can now see.

"I was totally blind in my right eye," she said, "and the vision in the other was just a blur."

While she was in a Leeds hospital waiting for an operation she met 62-year-old Mary.

She, too, was blind in one eye because of a brain tumour.

But the cornea – the eye's "lens" – was healthy and she decided to donate it to Angela.

Mary, of Airedale, West Yorkshire, said: "I realised that I could help a young woman who had never seen her children."

Angela said: "I can never thank Mary enough. It was a tremendous sacrifice for her." [. . .]

Angela was married in 1981 but later separated.

She said: "I managed somehow, but it was hard work fumbling with nappies and dealing with household chores."

"Everything was a terrible blur and I dreamed constantly of being able to see the children properly."

"Now my dream has come true, thanks to Mary."

After the operation Angela saw her children for the first time.

"It was the most magical moment of my life. I looked at their wonderful smiles and just broke down and wept."

"They look even lovelier than I had pictured. Now it's wonderful to watch their faces when I read them bedtime stories."

(from the *Daily Mirror*)

★ Find the five phrases in the text above. Put the numbers in the boxes to show the meaning of each phrase (one of the boxes needs two numbers).

1. partially blind
2. restore your sight
3. totally blind
4. a terrible blur
5. see properly

help you see again	2
see well	
not see very much	
see nothing	

10

18,000 kilometres away Brian Mason feels much the same. He's a 61-year-old grandfather from Greytown in the Wairarapa in New Zealand. He had been blind for 25 years.

And ever since [a] cornea transplant operation at Wellington Hospital, he has been opening his eyes to a new – and strange – world.

He recalls those first hours of sight: "I knew it was my wife, Fay, but she had got a lot older. I was stunned to see how beautiful my daughter had become. I looked in the mirror and I was shocked. Is that me? I asked."

From the hospital window he could see the colour of the grass – the colours of everything were so brilliant.

He saw strange objects swishing along the roads – modern cars.

He saw new high-rise buildings which he thought were toppling on to him.

Then it was back to his home . . . to lay eyes on old friends whom he had never seen [. . .]; to see, for the first time, his grandchildren.

Imagine going blind. Imagine then being able to see again like Angela and Brian and being asked by newspaper reporters how it felt. Perhaps you would answer them like Brian did.

"Tell your readers," he said, "I'm doing very well and the sky is still blue. As blue as ever."

(from *The New Zealand Herald*)

Mr Brian Mason and his wife, Fay, after his sight-restoring operation

Michelangelo, Martina and Marilyn

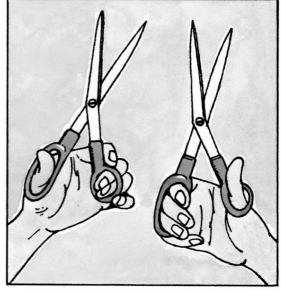

LIFE is easier if you're right-handed. You can open a can of tomatoes, use a pair of scissors or write a cheque without problems. People won't think that you're strange. And you'll be one of the 90% of people who use their right hand more than their left. Many animals are 'right-handed' or 'left-handed' too; what is interesting about human beings is that so many make the same choice – right-handedness. What makes us different?

In earlier times left-handed people were sometimes thought to be bad or even dangerous and were sometimes even killed. Even quite recently, children who wanted to use their left hands were taught to use their right instead. The teacher of King George VI of England (1895–1952) tied his left hand behind his back to make him use his right, and it was probably because of this that he had speech problems later in his life. However, modern ideas about how children use their hands are very different. Some doctors now think that the choice is made when babies are still very young. Look at this advice from a modern book for parents.

There is no natural law which states that one hand is superior to the other so it should never bother you if your child is left-handed. [. . .] You may think that by 'encouraging' your child to use his right hand instead of his left that you're doing him a favour for later life so that he'll never have to suffer the minor annoyances of right-handed potato peelers or scissors. You are not. And, what's more, you could well risk causing psychological side-effects like stuttering as well as reading and writing difficulties by altering what your baby's brain naturally wants to do.

(from *The Baby Care Book* by Dr Miriam Stoppard)

★ Which expresses best the meaning of the paragraph from *The Baby Care Book* – A, B or C?

A Don't worry if your child is left-handed and don't try to make him use his right hand – if you do, he may later have problems with speaking, reading and writing.

B If your child is left-handed help him to use his right hand more often – this will stop any problems later with speaking, reading and writing.

C It's better to be right-handed but don't worry if your child is left-handed. Give him right-handed things to use – this will help to change his brain.

But why is *anyone* left-handed? Why aren't we all right-handed – or perhaps 50% right-handed and 50% left? Psychologist Dr Marian Annett thinks that a long time ago people used both hands equally; what changed things was that human beings learned to speak.

The left hemisphere controls the right-hand side of the body and the right controls the left. Speech became connected to the left hemisphere of the brain; and as speech became more important, so the left hemisphere became more and more powerful. As the left hemisphere became more important, so the right-hand side of the body was used more; right-handedness became more common, and the functions of the right hemisphere became weaker. This means that left-handers are often slower to speak and read than right-handers. But left-handed people have advantages too.

At any given time, some 40 per cent of the top tennis players will be left-handed (Rod Laver, Martina Navratilova, John McEnroe and Jimmy Connors among them).

Left-handedness emerges most strikingly in the arts; back in the Renaissance, Leonardo da Vinci, Michelangelo and Hans Holbein were all notable left-handers. Add talented individuals from more recent times – such as Paul Klee, Charlie Chaplin, Lenny Bruce, Greta Garbo, Marilyn Monroe, Marcel Marceau, Jimi Hendrix [. . .] Shirley MacLaine, Robert de Niro and cartoonist Ronald Searle – and you are bound to conclude that lefties have as strong a set of advantages as handicaps.

(from *Company* magazine)

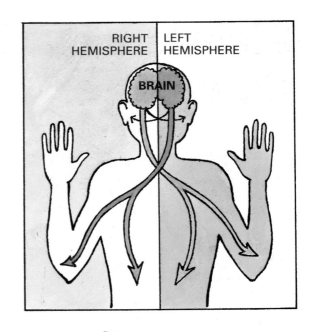

Four left-handers –Charlie Chaplin, Robert de Niro, Marilyn Monroe and Martina Navratilova

There are those who . . .

IT'S ONE of those games that people play all over the world – putting people into categories. 'Well of course,' we say, 'he's an American / the youngest in his family / one of those people who always arrive half an hour before the train leaves,' and everybody knows what we mean. Lots of us even enjoy finding out how we fit into other people's categories: open a magazine and try *not* to do the quiz that asks, 'Are you a good friend or a good lover?'

One form of this game is dividing people into two groups. Here are some of the things that writer Miles Kington came up with when he played with this idea.

There are two kinds of people in the world.

There are those who, when they collect their photographs from the chemist's shop, look at them all before they leave the shop, and those who wait till they get home.

There are those who take a bath to get themselves clean, and those who take a bath as a sort of cheap holiday.

There are those who, when writing a postcard, put the stamp on first, and there are those who put the name and address on first, and then find themselves sticking the stamp over half the name and address.

There are those who go to a dictionary to look a word up, and those who go to a dictionary and end up reading about every word except the word they went to look up.

There are people who kill spiders and people who rescue them.

There are those who kiss people on the cheek and those who hold out their cheeks to be kissed.

There are those who think that "modern" means something happening now and those who think that "modern" is something that happened just after World War II.

There are those who, when they eat fish, like the fish to look like a fish, and those who like it to look like little bits of meat, or even like potato crisps.

There are those whose main purpose in opening a present is to see what the present is, and those who are more interested in saving the wrapping paper for re-use.

There are those who pull plasters off very slowly and those who do it at one go.

There are those who always remember other people's birthdays and those who never even remember their own.

There are those who look at the dishes on a menu and those who look at the prices.

There are those who volunteer for the washing-up and those who prefer the drying.

There are those who can think of good ways to finish articles and those who simply write "To be continued".

(To be continued).

(adapted from an article by Miles Kington in *The Independent*)

Iceland

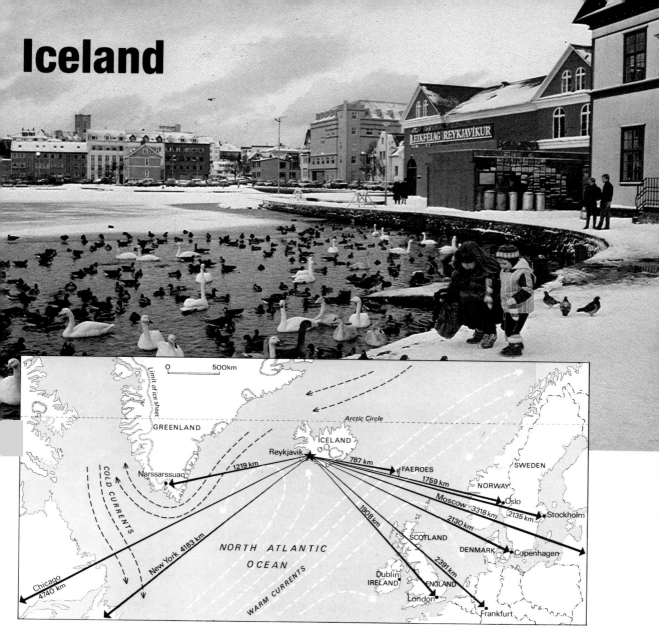

How do you imagine Iceland?

Here are some of the answers we had to this question.

'A little place, covered with ice, somewhere far away in the north.'
'Bare and rocky with steam and geysers coming out of the ground.'
'Quite green in parts with volcanoes and lava everywhere.'
'Wild and beautiful – I've always wanted to go there.'
'Lots of harbours and fish – fishermen.'
'Fire and snow, volcanoes and ice, the ground hot and bubbling.'
'White and blue, ice and cold.'

But this picture of Iceland is only partly true. First of all Iceland is not as far north as some people imagine, and it's bigger than many people think too.

Iceland is situated in the North Atlantic Ocean almost equidistant from New York and Moscow. It lies between 63° 24' and 66° 33'N, and between longitude 13° 30' and 24° 32'W and is the second-largest island in Europe. It is close to the Arctic Circle yet only one of its northerly islands actually lies inside it. The country has a total area of 103,000 sq km (39,796 sq miles) and a coastline of about 6,600km (3,700 miles). The island is 300km (190 miles) wide north to south, and 500km (300 miles) across from west to east.

(from *The Visitor's Guide to Iceland* by Don Philpott)

There is not as much ice in Iceland as people often imagine. Icecaps and glaciers cover only 11% of the country (about 11,000 sq km). Iceland is not as cold as people think either; in July the average temperature is about 9°C to 12°C, and the highest temperature ever recorded was a little more than 30°C. On the coast in the winter temperatures are about −2°C to 2°C, though it gets much colder inland. The lowest temperature recorded in the last 30 years was less than −15°C. Iceland gets a lot of rain with snow on high ground and in the north in the winter. It's also a windy place and the weather is very changeable.

A land of fire and water

Volcanoes and lava, geysers, pools of bubbling mud – think of Iceland and you probably think of things like these.

Strokkur, one of Iceland's most famous geysers; it can send a column of hot water 20m to 40m into the air.

A pool of hot bubbling mud in Námarskarað in the north-east of Iceland

below: Hekla, Iceland's most famous volcano, seen across the Thjórsá, Iceland's longest river

Midnight sun and winter nights

Because of Iceland's latitude, the days are very long in the summer and can be exceptionally short during winter. In Reykjavik for example, the longest day is nearly 21 hours long, but the shortest is just under 4 hours. In the north the summer sun hardly sets at all, with sunset after midnight in July. The amount of sunshine thus varies tremendously through the year; during the years of 1931–1960, Reykjavik had on average 1,249 hours of sunshine each year, but while there were 189 hours in July, December only enjoyed 8 hours.

(from *Iceland, the Visitor's Guide* by David Williams)

Iceland past and present

If you look at the kind of products that Iceland exports today – fish, meat and wool for example – it's easy to see that both the sea and the land are important to Icelanders. This has been true in fact since the time of the first Icelanders – Vikings from Norway who arrived in AD 874.

From 1262 to 1944 Iceland was ruled first by Norway and then by Denmark. Centuries of foreign rule, and such things as volcanoes and the weather, made life very difficult at times for the Icelanders; there was lots of hard work and little change. The situation began to improve during the nineteenth century. Then in 1944 Iceland became an independent republic; since that time it has become quite a rich country where the people enjoy having cars, modern houses and lots of electrical equipment.

Some things in the lives of the Icelanders have changed very little though – the Icelandic language for example. 700 years ago the stories called Sagas were first written down; these can still be read in the original language without much difficulty by Icelandic speakers today.

Some facts and figures

- The population of Iceland is 235,000.

- The capital city, Reykjavik, is the world's most northerly capital.

- The Althing, which first assembled in AD 930, is often called the first parliament in history.

- Vikings from Iceland discovered Greenland and America in the tenth and eleventh centuries.

- Some 600 different books are published in Iceland every year – that's a different book for approximately every 390 people in the country.

- The biggest glacier in Iceland, Vatnajökull, is also the biggest in Europe. The ice is more than 1000m thick in some parts and it is about 8,400 sq km in area.

- Hot water from under the ground gives Icelanders cheap electricity; it also gives central heating for their homes and for greenhouses where they grow salad vegetables and fruit – including bananas.

- If you're interested in a holiday in Iceland, there's lots to do: fishing, bird-watching, walking, climbing, skiing, camping, golf, horse riding . . . and swimming in pools of hot water.

★ Look back at the text to find these words. Then decide which group the words belong to – 'cold' or 'warm/hot'.

Cold		Warm/Hot
	steam	
	volcanoes	————
	lava	
	icecaps	
	glaciers	
————	snow	
	greenhouses	

18

Stephen's drawings

THIS IS St Paul's Cathedral, one of the most famous sights in London. Round the 300-year-old cathedral there are the streets and buildings of the commercial centre of London. It's a difficult subject for a picture but the artist, Stephen Wiltshire, has drawn something that Londoners can recognise immediately. One of the most interesting things about this picture, however, is that Stephen didn't draw it while looking at St Paul's or at a photograph of it; he drew it from memory. The drawing of Buckingham Palace below is another example of Stephen's work; this too was drawn from memory.

Stephen enjoys drawing buildings more than anything. After fifteen minutes in front of buildings like these he can go away and draw them, quickly and very accurately, from memory. What is perhaps more surprising is that Stephen was only eleven years old when he did these two drawings.

Not many children produce a book or have an exhibition of drawings at the age of eleven, but Stephen has done both. The drawings shown here

come from the book, which was the result of a BBC television programme. This programme was about the effects of autism, and Stephen was in it because he is both autistic and unusually good at drawing.

From a very young age autistic children have problems in their relationships with other people; one well-known sign of this is a problem with language. Most children learn to talk very early in life; they soon learn to use language to ask for things they want, to talk about their ideas and feelings, to ask questions and solve problems. Children who are autistic, however, don't begin learning to speak at the usual time; for reasons that aren't really understood they don't, or can't, use language as a door into the world of other people.

When Stephen began school at the age of four, he hardly ever looked at other people or tried to communicate with them. However, he was obviously interested in drawing and his teachers used this to help him. They worked hard to get Stephen to talk about his drawing. For a long time he said nothing, but one day he said, 'Paper?' This was the beginning. Stephen asked for things more often – and every time he did his teachers quickly responded. Slowly Stephen learned to use more words and to talk about his pictures. At the same time his drawings improved.

Language is still difficult for Stephen, but he is learning and he can now read. He will soon be going to his secondary school. He has visited the school and says he likes it, and his teachers are happy that he will do well there. Drawing continues to bring pleasure to him and, since the television programme and the book, to other people too. When Stephen was asked about this he said, 'I'm glad they like my drawings.' When you think that Stephen once could hardly communicate at all, what he says means a lot.

Stephen drawing the Houses of Parliament

(drawings and photo from *Drawings* by Stephen Wiltshire)

A bit of good luck – and a lot of bad

★ Read this with a dictionary.

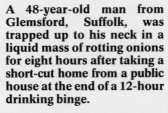

A 48-year-old man from Glemsford, Suffolk, was trapped up to his neck in a liquid mass of rotting onions for eight hours after taking a short-cut home from a public house at the end of a 12-hour drinking binge.

(from the *Western Mail*)

A Portuguese airliner had to be grounded in Lisbon for cleaning after eight gallons* of live maggots being taken by Welsh fishing team manager John Mayers to the world championships in Portugal broke loose from his hand luggage.

(from *The Western Daily Press*)

* *eight gallons:* about 36 litres

A pug dog named Paddington, wearing a £12,000 diamond necklace for a television commercial, wandered out of the studio in Calder City, California, while the humans involved were otherwise occupied. Five hours later, Paddington was found wandering three blocks away, still wearing the necklace. Bob Rosenberg, the advertising executive handling the commercial says that during the dog's absence "I aged 10 years".

(from *The Daily Telegraph*)

A python snake, left unattended in a Bremen flat while its owner went away for the weekend, turned on a bath tap and flooded homes below, police said yesterday. – Reuter

(from *The Guardian*)

Super-fit or super-mad?

AT THE beach recently my sister-in-law and I watched a swimmer come out of the water. He was wearing a wetsuit, and my sister-in-law knew immediately why he had been swimming there.

'Oh no,' she said, 'it must be triathlon time again. Hundreds of mad people running out of the water and jumping onto bicycles – it happens every year and I can't stand it.'

It made me think. My sister-in-law quite likes sport; she swims a lot and she's learning to windsurf. Perhaps she just dislikes the noise of the triathlon passing her house each year. But it's more likely that she, like lots of other people, can't understand why so many people are getting interested in this new sport.

It's true that every time somebody thinks of a new sport some love it and others hate it. When jogging became popular, for example, some believed it was great exercise, while others said it gave you heart attacks and did terrible things to the knees. The same kind of thing is said about the triathlon. The difference is that there are now people who do nothing but train for triathlons and compete in them. How did this all begin?

The sport began in Hawaii as recently as 1978. A group of sportsmen were arguing about which kind of athlete was the fittest – a cyclist, a runner or a swimmer. It seemed an impossible question to answer until one of them, an officer in the US Navy called John Collings, made a suggestion. There were already three big races in Hawaii, one each for swimmers, cyclists and runners; if you joined all three races together, he said, you could see which kind of athlete was the fittest.

This was the beginning of the famous Hawaiian triathlon called the Ironman. Athletes in the Ironman swim for 2.4 miles, cycle for 112 miles, and then run a marathon – 26.2 miles. 15 people competed in the first Ironman in 1978, and the winner took nearly 12 hours to finish the race.

Now there are short, middle and long distance triathlons as well as the ultra-distance triathlons like the Ironman. Thousands of people train for and compete in triathlons; just six years after the first Ironman, the 1984 race attracted 1,153 competitors. The sport has travelled to all parts of Europe, South Africa, Brazil, Australia and New Zealand, and it may be included in the Olympic Games before long. One thing that hasn't changed, however, is the order of the three different parts of the triathlon: usually swimming is first, then cycling, then running. This is mainly for safety reasons: a tired runner can walk or stop if necessary, but a tired swimmer might drown.

Here are some of the reasons why people enjoy triathlons:

- It's good exercise for the whole body. Swimming gives you strong arms and shoulders, running gives you strong legs, but only triathlon training develops every part of the body.

- It's a sport for both men and women; nearly all triathlons have been open to both sexes. And it's not just for young people: athletes in their thirties often do better than those in their teens or twenties.

- You don't need a lot of equipment – a bicycle, shoes and shorts to run in, and a swimming costume – and it doesn't have to be expensive either.

- The only rule in triathlons is that you have to swim, run and cycle the different distances alone and without help.

- You can find the kind of triathlon that suits you. Beginners, or people who can't spend much time training, may choose a short race that's over in an hour or two; others who are strong rather than fast may prefer an ultra that takes 10 or 15 hours to finish.

It all sounds fine. But triathletes do sound a little mad. Take Dave Scott, who has won the Hawaiian Ironman several times, each time with a new world record. He trains for five to seven hours a day, much of the time alone. He needs 5,000 calories a day to do this (more than twice as many as an average adult) and has been known to eat 17 bananas at one sitting. It must be great to be the best in your sport, but surely there is more to life than running, cycling and swimming alone all day and then eating bananas.

Perhaps this is what makes people uneasy about sports like the triathlon. No doubt people will always want to go a little bit faster, a little bit further, or a little bit longer, and most of us admire athletes who make new world records. It's when you read about athletes who have nothing but sport in their lives that you begin to wonder. Do they ever have time to play the piano? have a drink with a friend? go and see a film? Now that it's possible to compete in a triathlon that lasts for three days, with distances twice as long as the Hawaiian Ironman, we'll probably start to hear about people who train for 12 hours a day and have to eat every two hours to get enough food into their bodies. Personally, on triathlon day I'll be inside the house with my sister-in-law until they've all gone past on their bicycles. Then we'll take the dog for a walk (1.2 miles).

One triathlete running – hundreds beginning the swim

What to do when someone's choking

CHOKING happens when food or drink, or anything else, goes down the windpipe instead of the food passage. When the windpipe is completely blocked, the choking person will not be able to speak, cough or breathe and will quickly go blue in the face. First try to get the obstruction out with your finger. If you can't get it out, immediately hit the casualty between the shoulders with the heel of your hand. Hold the casualty as shown below.

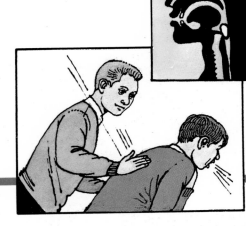

Baby: slap quickly between the shoulders four times.

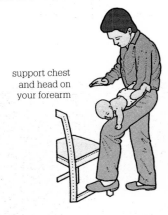

support chest and head on your forearm

Older children and adults: treat them in whatever position they are in. Slap swiftly between shoulders up to four times.

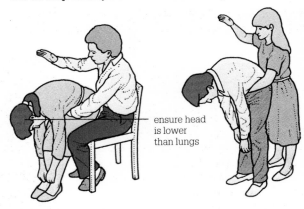

ensure head is lower than lungs

Small child: slap hard between shoulders four times.

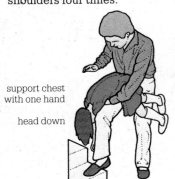

support chest with one hand

head down

Abdominal thrust
If the obstruction has not been dislodged by the method described, try to remove it with an abdominal thrust. **Do this only as a last resort if all other methods have failed.**

1   Stand the casualty up and stand behind him.

24

2   Put your arms round him. Clench one fist and put it, thumb inwards, between the navel and the ribcage. Clasp the fist with your other hand and give a quick, hard squeeze. Push the clenched fist inwards and slightly upwards.

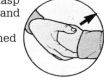

★ Match the words with their meanings (in this text). Notice that you need to use one meaning twice.

casualty — hit
obstruction — get (the food etc.) out
slap — hand
dislodge — the choking person
remove — food etc. in the windpipe
fist

Abdominal thrust for children
1   Sit the child on your lap. Support the back with one hand. Clench the fist of the other hand and put it, thumb inwards, between the navel and the ribcage. Press the clenched fist inwards and upwards. Don't use as much force as you would for an adult.

(from *First Aid* by Ruth Thomson)

Showers, flying machines and phonographs

IN THE period between 1865 and 1900 both the typewriter and the telephone were invented. Before the end of the century people drove cars for the first time, travelled by train and saw moving pictures at the cinema; X-rays were discovered and messages were sent by wireless telegraph across the Channel between England and France. Not all of the inventions of that time were successful however, and many of them – as you can see here – looked very strange. Yet if there hadn't been any nineteenth century inventors with strange ideas, our lives would be very different today.

The 'velocipede shower bath' shown here had a seat and pedals like a bicycle. The pedals operated a small pump which forced water from a tank up a tube and out over the person having the shower. For a hot shower, a heater could be placed under the tank.

The inventor of the velocipede shower bath naturally hoped it would be very popular. It wasn't, but it did work. The 'natural flying machine', for

The velocipede shower bath, Scientific American, 1897

*A natural flying machine,
Scientific American, 1865*

obvious reasons, wouldn't have worked. This machine was suggested to the *Scientific American* in 1865 by a reader. He thought that ten brown eagles wearing special jackets could carry an adult through the air. The person in the machine would control the height above ground by pulling strings attached to the birds' wings. The direction of the machine would also be controlled by strings pulling the birds' heads one way or the other.

The terrifying invention at the top of the next page was shown in the French scientific journal *La Nature* in 1891. The idea was to drop the metal shell, with 15 people in it, into a pool of water under the Eiffel Tower in Paris. The shell would fall about 300m. *La Nature* said that the speed of

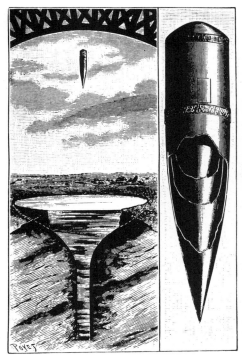

A machine for sensational emotions, La Nature, 1891

the shell would be '84 yards per second, corresponding to about 172 miles per hour, a speed at which no human being has ever travelled.' (76.8m per second, or 276.7km per hour.) Notice that there is no window in the cabin of the shell, though there is an electric light. Notice also the springs under the floor of the cabin. The inventor thought people would enjoy the feeling of dropping through the air at great speed for a few seconds. Luckily, perhaps, he never found out if this was true, because the 'machine for sensational emotions' was never built.

Thomas Edison's most famous invention is probably the light-bulb; his favourite though was the phonograph. The phonograph, he said, would replace shorthand typists and it would be used to teach languages. He believed that a phonograph and a clock could be used together so that the clock would actually say what the time was. He thought that people would send phonographic records instead of letters and that they would record the voices of their children and the last words of the dying. Edison also believed that people would listen to world-famous musicians on phonographs in their own homes.

People have forgotten the 'velocipede shower bath' and many other strange nineteenth century vehicles and contraptions. They have largely forgotten Edison's phonograph too, but it was actually an early kind of record or cassette player. So, although we don't use phonographs any more, Edison was right – in a way – about his strange nineteenth century invention.

A cornet player recording on Edison's phonograph, La Nature, 1889

Some other kind of people

An American Indian hunting buffalo

IN THE last years of the nineteenth century, a young American Indian called Buffalo Child Long Lance was growing up in North America. His tribe, the Blackfeet, lived in an area between Montana in the USA and Alberta in Canada; here they followed the buffalo, which they hunted for its skins and meat. Like all the boys in the tribe, Long Lance learned to ride, hunt, fight and dance.

No white people came to this remote part of North America until the 1880s – but when they did, the lives of the Blackfeet began to change greatly. Instead of hunting buffalo, Long Lance went to school and then fought as a Canadian soldier in the 1914–18 war. After the war he became a newspaper journalist.

Long Lance also wrote a book about his life and the life of his people. In the book he tells of an early meeting between the Blackfeet and the white man. The Blackfeet had heard that they could trade their buffalo skins for gunpowder and food at

the white man's trading post. On the way there they met another tribe of Indians called the Suksiseoketuk, who already traded with the white man. The Blackfeet were very interested

Blackfoot Indians trading

in what the Suksiseoketuk chief told them, because they had only seen white men from a distance, and they had never seen white women or children.

He told us to beware of his food; as it would make our teeth come out. He told us about the bread and the sweets which the white man ate, and he pulled up his upper lip and said: 'Wambadahka – Behold – my teeth are good, and so are the teeth of all our old people; but behold,' he said, walking over to a young boy and pulling up his lip, 'behold, these teeth of the young people are not good – too much white man's food. Our people, like yours, never used to die until they were over a hundred years old. Now, since we started to eat that white man's food we are sick all of the time. We keep getting worse and soon it will kill us all.'

The Suksiseoketuk chief also told them not to wash their hair with the white man's soap, or, like the white man, they would soon have no hair on the top of their heads. Then he told the Blackfeet that some of his men would go with them to the white man's trading post. After six days' walking they arrived near the trading post, and some of the Blackfeet went out to hunt for food.

★ Look at the paragraph between ▶ and ◀ again. When you see 'they' or 'them' decide if it means 'the Blackfeet' or 'the other people'. Put *B* (Blackfeet) or *O* (other people) in the spaces on the right.

▶ While they were out they came upon a cabin, and they saw six long-haired people with light skin, going in and out of this place. Our warriors sat down and watched them and tried to figure out what they were; they had never seen any people like them before. They were not Indians and they were not white men; so one of our warriors, Big Darkness, said that they must be the white man's woman – their wives – white women! They had never seen any white women before; so they all agreed that that must be what they were. ◀

they *B* they *B* they *B*

them......
they...... they...... them......
They...... they *O*
they *O*
They......
they......
they......

But when they came back to camp and told the others about it, another of our warriors, Sun Calf, who had seen the women, changed his mind and said that he did not believe they were white women after all; they were 'some other kind of people', he said.

Some agreed with Big Darkness, and some with Sun Calf, and an argument started. Finally their chief decided that some of the men should go and capture one of these people and then everybody could look and decide. When night came, Big Darkness, Sun Calf and eight other Blackfeet went to the cabin and came back with one of the strange people – who, naturally, was very frightened.

The argument began again. It became so noisy that some of the Suksiseoketuk Indians came to see what was happening.

They stopped and listened for a moment, and then they began to laugh. They laughed for a long time before they would tell us what they were laughing at. And then one of them said:

'Inexperienced Blackfeet! It is neither a white woman nor any kind of being that you have ever seen before. It is a man from across the Minne-Tonka, and he waved his arm towards the Pacific Ocean.

It was a Chinaman!

(from *Long Lance – the Autobiography of a Blackfoot Indian Chief* by Chief Buffalo Child Long Lance)

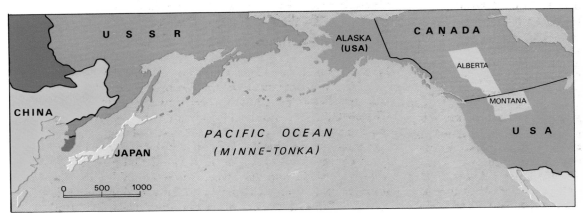

Is fashion as silly as it looks?

FOR ME the answer to this question is, 'Well, sometimes – yes.' Look at the picture. It was taken at an 'important' hairdressing competition in London in 1987. The hairdresser has probably spent hours on the young woman's hair. No doubt he hopes he'll win a prize – and perhaps he will. And look at the woman. What's on top of her head seems to be more important than what's inside it. What's worse is that maybe this doesn't worry her.

What about men? John Richmond is a young fashion designer from Britain.

John Richmond [. . .] **says he prefers his own designs but does buy the odd pair of cycling shorts or something by** Vivienne Westwood. **Also likes** Yohji Yamamoto, Jean Paul Gaultier **and shirts by** John Smedley.

He's successful and he can make money designing clothes – clothes that many people might think were silly. He's also quite serious about his designs; as we've seen, he likes wearing them himself. But look at his shirt. Even if it's just for parties, how do you hold a drink when you're wearing it?

One thing I do understand about fashion is that it's expensive. If you're a fashionable woman, of course, it costs you more and it's harder work – hair or skirts have to be longer or shorter, for example. For some reason men don't have the problem of short trousers one year and long ones the next.

But *is* fashion really as silly as it seems? Cathy Elston is a fashion designer and illustrator who has taught fashion design; I asked her what she thought.

Cathy agrees that fashion makes us want things we don't need:

'The fashion industry certainly encourages us to want more than we need, which is one aspect of the industry that is very disturbing.'

(from *The Observer Magazine*, August 1987)

But this doesn't mean that fashion is silly.

'For a start, the fashion industry is one of the world's biggest industries, providing work for millions of people.'

Cathy also believes that clothes help us to say what kind of people we are and that they make the world interesting. People enjoy this – and that's a good thing.

'Clothes provide us with an environment of moving colour and form; not only that, people enjoy thinking about what to wear. Without fashion what *would* people wear? Uniforms would take away our freedom of choice and I do not believe the world would be a happier place if we all dressed the same.

Although it might have been true in the past, to suggest that women today dress only to please men and think that only clothes are important undermines women's intelligence and is sexist. More than half the world's fashion designers are women; besides, men are as fashion-conscious as women.'

Cathy thinks that fashions now give us more choice than there has ever been before, and she says:

'Changing attitudes give us the freedom to wear whatever we like.'

Perhaps she's right, and it's not always a choice between looking silly and looking old-fashioned. Maybe it's possible to have men's *and* women's clothes that are comfortable and sensible but that also look good. Have a look at some of Cathy's work.

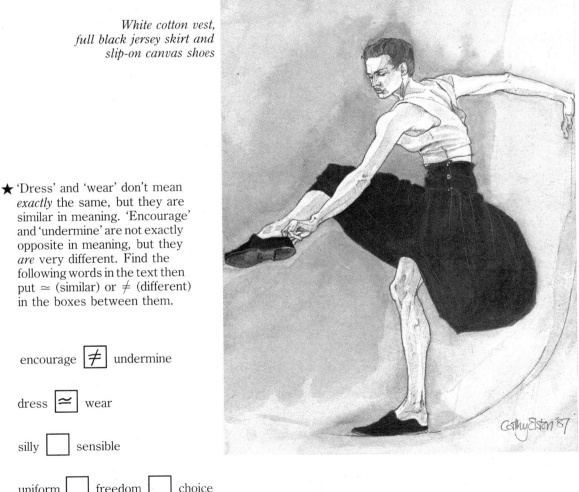

White cotton vest, full black jersey skirt and slip-on canvas shoes

★ 'Dress' and 'wear' don't mean *exactly* the same, but they are similar in meaning. 'Encourage' and 'undermine' are not exactly opposite in meaning, but they *are* very different. Find the following words in the text then put ≃ (similar) or ≠ (different) in the boxes between them.

encourage ≠ undermine

dress ≃ wear

silly ⬜ sensible

uniform ⬜ freedom ⬜ choice

fashion-conscious ⬜ fashionable ⬜ old-fashioned

31

Floating in the air

★ Use a dictionary to look up as many of the <u>underlined</u> words as you need to.

Mike Moore usually knows where he's going to start work but he can never be completely sure where he'll finish. He may not know if he can work at all until a few minutes before he begins. Most people would probably prefer a more <u>predictable</u> job than his, but after 20 years Mike still loves being a hot air balloonist.

When Mike began flying balloons in the late 1960s, it was a very new sport; there were only about three balloons in Britain at that time. Mike joined some other university students who wanted to buy a balloon together.

'None of the group had ever actually seen one, though we'd seen pictures in magazines. We fell in love with the idea of ballooning and then had to find out who could teach us and how it was done.

When we finally took delivery of our balloon nine months later, we didn't know which part of it was what. We put it all out on the <u>ground</u> and said, "Well this is obviously the basket and this is the envelope, this must be the burner – and how does it work?"'

Mike remembers very clearly the first time he flew.

'I had never been off the ground at all in anything, so my first view of the ground from the air was from a balloon. Actually the one thing I saw much of was the bottom of the basket, because I just crouched down and <u>refused</u> to stand up.'

But the next flight was less frightening, and Mike decided to have lessons. After a year he got

Mike at work

his licence to fly balloons. Now, 20 years later, he has different problems to deal with.

'It can get repetitive. When somebody flies for the first time it is absolutely <u>enchanting</u>. But you yourself can get bored with making the same flights in the same areas because you always go the same way.

So I do try to do other things too. I like balloon competitions and unusual flights (though it took me 15 years to find the time to fly the Channel*, which I did a couple of years ago). We go in for long flights now for fun – my personal record is 90 miles.'

Mike has taken groups of tourists

*Channel: the sea between England and France

sightseeing in his balloon in Spain and Kenya, and he also teaches other balloonists to fly and examines them for their licences. At the moment he is running a competition for balloonists, doing the work on the ground that makes the competition possible.

Sometimes Mike flies alone and sometimes he takes passengers. Flying on your own can actually be rather lonely; flying in a big balloon with perhaps 12 passengers almost always brings problems – someone who can't climb into the basket because of their wooden leg, for example, or someone who's worried about getting back before a certain time. But what he likes most is flying with three or four people, because with a small group like this it's easier to relax and there's time to talk.

There are probably about 40 full-time professional balloonists in Britain today. So what kind of person makes a good one? In Mike's opinion, it's someone who can decide things quickly on his own, sometimes in difficult situations. It's someone who can change his plans to suit the weather and who can deal with passengers when a flight has to be cancelled.

In Mike's experience people nearly always enjoy ballooning, though he remembers one passenger who didn't.

'I once took off with four in the basket including myself and after about five minutes I looked round and could only see two people. In fact the other passenger was down on the floor of the basket – just like I had been on my first flight. Later he got up, but after a while I began to worry about a vibration I could feel in the balloon. Then I realised it was his knees knocking together.'
People don't know very much about ballooning, Mike often finds.

'Many times I've taken off with a crowd of people in the balloon

Balloons at Bristol's Balloon Fiesta

and a voice says after a few minutes, "How are we steering this?" You can't steer a balloon – that isn't what ballooning is.

People often ask me if it's cold. No it isn't – not for the first three or four thousand feet. Because you're travelling with the wind, and don't feel the wind, you actually feel warmer.

It's unpredictable. There aren't many people who really enjoy that; usually they're too worried about the time and about getting back for dinner. Balloonists don't usually think like that – they *like* unexpected things happening. Once you start enjoying the unexpected, ballooning becomes a sport which can last you a lifetime.'
No doubt this is why Mike is always trying something new.

'In 1987 I flew the largest balloon in Europe to set a world record for the number of passengers carried. I held the record for a week – 35 passengers. The balloon was 850,000 cubic feet; the normal size of a balloon is less than a quarter of that.'
He is often asked to test balloons made in special shapes, and in 1987 he delivered one of these balloons to Florida in the United States. It was in the shape of Mickey Mouse.

'It had lovely great big ears, a wonderful nose, and those world-famous eyes. I went with it on the plane and delivered it to the people in Disneyworld who were going

Mickey Mouse – and friend – by the Enchanted Castle at Disneyworld

⋙➤

to be flying it. While I was there we did the weather forecast from Mickey on TV – 'Good Morning America' – in front of 125 million people. I also flew the President of the Disney Corporation over the Magic Kingdom and we were given free passes all week long to Disneyworld.'

After 20 years of ballooning, is there anything Mike still wants to do?

'I want to develop the experience for other people in an interesting way. What I don't want is ballooning to become mechanical, like regular scheduled flying. Floating in a balloon is magic and the only thing I want to do is keep it that way.'

Three love poems

Red and white roses

There's my sweetheart on the hill,
The red rose and the white;
The red rose drops its petals,
But the white rose is my sweetheart.

(A traditional Welsh poem, perhaps seventeenth century, translated by Kenneth Hurlstone Jackson.)

Love me

Love me
but do not come too near
leave room for love
to laugh at its happiness
always let some of my blond hair
be free

(By Maria Wine, a Swedish poet who was born in 1912. This translation is by Nadia Christensen.)

I through blue sky

I
Through
Blue
Sky
Fly
To
You
Why?
Sweet
Love
Feet
Move
So
Slow

(The author of this unusual love poem is not known.)

Mum's snake

'I HAVE lived a very good life, it has been very rich and full. I have been very fortunate and I am thrilled by it all when I look back.' With these words, at the age of 83, Bert Facey finished the story of his life. At first 'fortunate' seems like a surprising word to choose, for his life certainly wasn't easy. In 1903, when he was just eight years old, he was working for his living on a farm in Western Australia. Later he and two of his brothers went to fight in the 1914–18 War; the two brothers were killed, and Bert himself was so badly injured that the doctors said he would live for only two years. However, for ten years after the war he had a successful farm. Then, in the great Depression of the 1930s, he lost it.

But despite difficulties like these Bert thought his life was a good one. He had a long happy marriage and seven children; he also had lots of different jobs, which was something he enjoyed. And at the very end of his life his book *A Fortunate Life* was published and it made him famous – a great thrill for a man who had never been to school and who had taught himself to read and write.

★ Look at these words from the text above; does each word mean something good or something bad?

	rich	
	full	
————————	fortunate	
GOOD	thrilled	BAD
	injured	
	successful	
	lost	
	difficulties	⟫⟫→

Bert in 1914, aged 20 . . .

. . . and in 1981, aged 87

At the time of this story he was 12 years old; he was working for a Mr and Mrs Phillips, who he called 'Frank' and 'Mum', helping them with their animals. They were kind people and looked after him well, giving him good food and buying him extra clothes. Their farm was 30 miles from Narrogin, the nearest town.

One day Frank and Bert were coming back to the house for lunch when they heard Mum give a terrible scream.

She came running out of the lavatory* holding up her dress with one hand and clutching her bottom with the other. She was yelling out loudly, 'I've been bitten by a snake!' Frank and I ran to her and helped her inside the house.

Frank took her into the bedroom and told me to run over to the Connors' place and get Jack to bring his horse and sulky† to take Mum to the doctor. It was a little over two miles to Jack's and I ran all the way.

Jack, the Phillips' nearest neighbour, quickly put the horse in the sulky and drove to the Phillips' house. The two men put Mum into the sulky and began the long drive to the doctor at Narrogin, leaving Bert to look after the farm and the animals. The first thing he did was to go and look for the snake.

After they had gone I got a nice handy stick, about four feet long, and went into the lavatory after the snake. This lavatory was mainly used by Mum; I never used it and Frank only sometimes. It was made of galvanised iron and had a small hole cut out at the back to allow Mum to slide the pan in. (The pan was an old kerosene tin cut to fit). A bag was hung on the back wall to cover the hole. With the stick I approached the lavatory, carefully looking in and around, but I couldn't see any sign of the snake. I lifted the bag up very slowly (I was scared stiff), then I heard something move. Quickly I dropped the bag and jumped back. Then all was quiet again. I lifted the bag once more. This time I noticed some feathers, and as I lifted the bag further, more feathers came into view. All at once I knew what had bitten Mum.

Bert laughed till he cried. A hen had made a nest by the lavatory pan, and that's what had bitten Mum.

They were away for nearly four days. When they came home [. . .] I asked her how she was and she said that the doctor had said that he didn't think it was a snake that had bitten her and if it was it wasn't poisonous. She asked if I'd looked around the lavatory for the snake and I said that I had and that I had found the thing that had bitten her. I said that it was still in the lavatory and I offered to show it to her.

We went to the lavatory and I lifted up the bag. She looked under and exclaimed, 'Good God. No!' [. . .] She stood for a while and seemed to be thinking, or working something

out in her mind. Then suddenly she said, 'Did you have any visitors while we were away or see anyone?' I said, 'No.' 'Well,' she said, 'don't you say anything, not even to Frank or anybody, about this. [. . .] Bert, I love you, but if you tell anyone about this I'll kill you.' I promised not to tell anyone. Nothing more was said about the 'snake bite'.

(from *A Fortunate Life* by A.B. Facey)

lavatory: toilet
†*sulky:* small cart with two wheels

Dressing for the disco

★ Try this puzzle.

The five Golightly sisters – Amelia, Beatrice, Clarity, Dorothy and Emily – go out a lot together to dances and discos. Since they're not very well off, they usually share their clothes, which gives them a bigger choice of things to wear. They have 12 frocks between them, four pink, four mauve and four scarlet. Luckily they are all the same size, so if they're going out together the only thing they have to agree about is who wears which colour.

Last Friday night the girls all wanted to go to the disco. They got out all the frocks and went from one to another, trying to decide which to wear, and looking to see what the other sisters were choosing. Finally they managed to come to a decision that they all liked.

Emily decided to choose between pink and scarlet.

Amelia, Beatrice and Emily decided that they would each wear a different colour.

If Clarity and Emily chose the same colour, Amelia and Dorothy would also wear the same colour.

If Dorothy and Emily wore the same colour, Amelia and Clarity would choose the same colour.

If Amelia and Clarity chose the same colour, Beatrice and Dorothy would also choose the same colour.

If Beatrice did not wear scarlet, either Amelia or Clarity (or both) were going to choose it.

If Dorothy did not choose pink, then pink would be worn by Amelia or Clarity.

As it turned out, two of the girls chose mauve.

What were the colours chosen by each of the Golightly girls for the frocks they wore to the disco?

(from *Diversions – Exercises for Mental Athletes* by Wilkins)

Hic . . . hic

YOU'VE just eaten a sandwich, rather fast, and you've hurried back to work. You sit down at your desk and 'Hic . . . hic' – you've got hiccups. What do you do about it? Hiccups can be difficult to stop; perhaps you've tried some of these cures.
- Drinking water slowly.
- Drinking water – from the other side of the glass.
- Standing on your head.
- Sucking sugar or a sweet.
- Breathing in and out of a paper bag (not a plastic one) for a minute or two.
- Holding your breath for a minute.

According to the *Family Medical Encyclopedia*, drinking water or holding your breath may help, but breathing into a bag won't. Other cures for hiccups (or 'hiccoughs' or 'singultus') may *seem* to work, but in fact they probably just help you to think of something else until your hiccups stop. None of these cures, however, helped Charles Osborne.

> The longest recorded attack of hiccoughs or singultus is that afflicting Charles Osborne (b. 1894) of Anthon, Iowa, USA, for the past 65 years from 1922. He [. . .] has hiccoughed about 430 million times in the interim period. He has been unable to find a cure, but has led a reasonably normal life in which he has had two wives and fathered eight children. He has admitted, however, that he cannot keep in his false teeth. In July 1986 he was reported to be hiccing at 20–25 per minute from his earlier high of 40.

(from *The Guinness Book of Records*)

Men and women

★ Read this with a dictionary.

The intelligence of woman is inferior to that of man, and every woman who tries to deny it proves it.
(Countess Diane of Poitiers (1499–1566) mistress of Henry II of France.)

A woman is always buying something.
(Ovid (43 BC–AD 17), Roman poet.)

Women are nothing but machines for producing children.
(Napoleon Bonaparte (1769–1821), French Emperor.)

Women are like elephants to me; I like to look at them, but I wouldn't want to own one.
(W.C. Fields (1879–1946), American film actor.)

I hate women because they always know where things are.
(James Thurber (1894–1964), American humorist.)

A woman's mind is like spring weather.
(Japanese proverb.)

Women are a trouble and a worry. (Arab proverb.)

A wife's advice is of little value, but he who does not take it is a fool. (Spanish proverb.)

If you want to understand man, study woman.
(French proverb.)

Love enters a man through his eyes; a woman through her ears.
(Polish proverb.)

Every woman should marry – and no man.
(Benjamin Disraeli (1804–81), British Prime Minister and novelist.)

If you want peace in your house, do what your wife wants.
(African proverb.)

The great truth is that women actually like men, and men can never believe it.
(Isabel Paterson (died 1961), Canadian writer.)

Woman to man is either a god or a wolf.
(John Webster (1580–1625), English dramatist.)

The only problem with women is men.

(Kathie Sarachild, contemporary American feminist.)

The more I see of men, the more I like dogs.

(*attributed to:* Madame de Sévigné (1626–96), French writer and
Madame De Staël (1766–1817), French writer.)

What is better than wisdom? Woman. And what is better than a good woman? Nothing.

(Geoffrey Chaucer (1340–1400), English writer.)

Equality is a myth – women are better.

(Graffito, London, 1980.)

Men are those creatures with two legs and eight hands.

(Jayne Mansfield (1932–67), American film actress.)

The majority of husbands remind me of an orang-utang trying to play the violin.

(Honoré de Balzac (1799–1850), French writer.)

When a man gets up to speak, people listen, then look. When a woman gets up, people look; *then, if they like what they see, they* listen.   (Pauline Frederick (1883–1938), American actress.)

Women want mediocre men, and men are working hard to be as mediocre as possible.

(Margaret Mead (1901–78), American anthropologist.)

How a little love and good company improves a woman!

(George Farquhar (1678–1707) English dramatist.)

A wife is not an instrument that can be hung against the wall when you have played on it.   (Russian proverb.)

If you want a speech to be made, ask a man. If you want something done, ask a woman.

(Margaret Thatcher (born 1925), British Prime Minister.)

I love men like some people like good food or wine.

(Germaine Greer (born 1939), Australian feminist.)

A woman is the only thing I am afraid of that I know will not hurt me.   (Abraham Lincoln (1809–65), US President.)

Men are people, just like women.

(Fenella Fielding (born 1934), Anglo-Rumanian actress.)

Maui's fish – or, where New Zealand comes from

BECAUSE New Zealand is in the southern hemisphere and most New Zealanders speak English as their first language, people often think it is near Australia. New Zealand *was* once part of eastern Australia – but that, of course, was millions of years ago. Since then New Zealand has moved south-east and it is now some 2,000 kilometres from Australia. Some time around AD 900 the Maori people arrived in their canoes on the coast of the North Island. They have a different story of where New Zealand comes from.

The hero of this story is a young man called Maui. Like any young Maori man he spent a lot of time catching birds and fish, and he was very clever at it. He could also do magic – he could change himself into a bird, for instance. His cleverness and magic used to annoy his older brothers, however, and when they went fishing they wouldn't take Maui with them.

This meant that he had to stay at home with his wives and children, with nothing to do, and listen to his wives complaining about the lack of fish to eat.

'Oh stop it, you women,' he said one day when their grumbling had got on his nerves. 'What are you fussing about? Haven't I done all manner of things by my enchantments*? Do you think a simple thing like catching a few fish is beyond me? I'll *go* out fishing and I'll catch a fish so big that you won't be able to eat it all before it goes bad.' He felt better when he had said this, and went off to a place where women were not allowed, and sat down to make himself a fish-hook.

Some of Maui's magic came to him from the jaw-bone of Muri ranga whenua. Muri was his old grandmother and she had given him the jawbone – and its magic powers – out of her own mouth.

* *enchantments*: magic

Maui receives Muri's jawbone

Maui used a piece of Muri's jawbone to make his fish-hook. When he had finished it he went down to the beach and hid himself under the floor of his brothers' canoe.

Early the next day his four brothers came with food and fishing gear; they pushed out to sea and had been paddling for some time before Maui came out of his hiding place.

All four of them felt like turning back at once, but Maui by his enchantments made the sea stretch out between their canoe and the land [. . .] There was not much point in objecting, so they resumed their paddling, and when they reached the place where they usually fished, one of them went to put the stone anchor overboard. 'No, no, not yet!' cried Maui. 'Better to go much further out.'

This happened several times, but each time his brothers wanted to stop Maui told them to go further out. At last they arrived at a place where Maui said there would be lots of fish.

It was exactly as he had said it would be. Their lines were hardly over the side before they all caught fish. [Soon] they had so many that it would have been unsafe to catch more, for the canoe was now getting low in the water. So they suggested going back.

'Wait on,' said Maui, 'I haven't tried my line yet.'

'Where did *you* get a hook?' they asked.

'Oh, I have one of my own,' said Maui. So the brothers knew for certain now that there was going to be trouble, as they had feared. They told him to hurry and throw his line over.

Maui tied the hook to a fishing-line and then asked his brothers for some bait to put on the hook, but they would not give him any. So he punched his own nose and put some of his blood on the hook. Singing a magic song to the north-east and the south-east winds, he dropped the hook and line over the side of canoe.

Down, down it sank, and when it was at the bottom Maui lifted it slightly and it caught on something which at once pulled very hard. Maui pulled also, and hauled in a little of his line. The canoe heeled over, and was shipping water fast. 'Let it go!' cried the frightened brothers, but Maui [. . .] would not let go.

What Maui had caught was both a fish – and not a fish. The hook was in the roof of the house of Tonganui, who lived at the bottom of the sea and whose name means 'Great South'. Maui had pulled it up almost to the surface of the water when, like a fish, it dived down again to the bottom. Maui sang the magic song that makes heavy things light and started pulling again.

At length there appeared beside them the gable and thatched roof of the house of Tonganui, and not only the house, but a huge piece of the land attached to it. The brothers wailed, and beat their heads, as they saw that Maui had fished up land, Te Ika a Maui, the Fish of Maui. And there were houses on it, and fires burning, and people.

Maui pulls up his fish

41

Maui told his brothers that he had to go back to their village but that he would return.

'Now while I'm away,' he said, 'show some common sense and don't be impatient. Don't eat food till I come back, and whatever you do don't start cutting up the fish until I have found a priest and made an offering to the gods [...] When I get back it will be all right to cut him up, and we'll share him out equally then. What we cannot take with us will keep until we come back for it.'

Maui then returned to their village. But as soon as his back was turned his brothers did the very things that he had told them not to. They began to eat food [...] And they started to scale the fish and cut bits off it.

(adapted from *Maori Myths and Tribal Legends* by Antony Alpers)

The gods were angry that they had not been given any of the fish first and they made the fish of Maui jump and turn angrily in the water. And that is why there are mountains in the North Island of New Zealand, because when the sun came up in the morning, it changed the angry fish into land. And the South Island? That is the canoe. The cape at Heretaunga is the fish-hook and, some people say, Stewart Island is the stone anchor of the canoe.

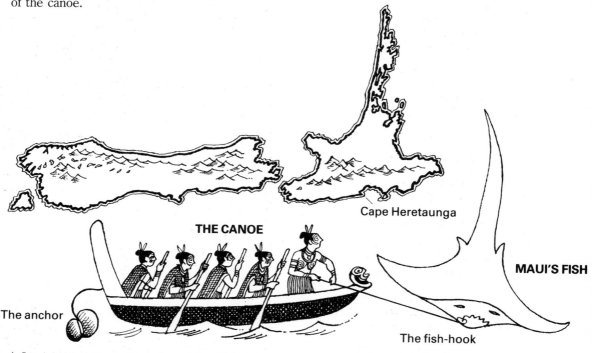

Cape Heretaunga

THE CANOE

MAUI'S FISH

The anchor

The fish-hook

★ Look back at the extracts from *Maori Myths and Tribal Legends*. Then number the following sentences to show the correct order.

◯ Maui's brothers tell him to stop, but he keeps pulling in his line.

◯ Maui tells his brothers to wait till he comes back, but they don't.

◯ Tired of his family's complaints, Maui decides to go fishing.

◯ They find that Maui's fish-hook has caught land.

◯ Maui's brothers catch lots and lots of fish – and then Maui starts fishing.

② Maui makes his brothers go a long way out to sea.

Marion throws away £23,000

MOVING house cost Bath business executive Marion Greene a £3,500 mink coat and £20,000 worth of jewellery.

For she put them in a plastic bin liner, and they were collected by the dustmen. The bag was then put through a shredder with other rubbish.

Miss Greene, aged 29, was moving from Fairford Avenue, Bath, to a new home in Briar Close, Frome, two weeks ago and packed all her belongings into bin liners.

But she only discovered what she had done when she went to find her coat to wear to a Christmas party.

Mistake

The bag with the £3,500 mink, £4,000 gold Rolex watch, £2,000 diamond and emerald earrings, a diamond and sapphire ring and assortment of other jewellery had gone.

"I had several lots of stuff for the binmen, I must have made a mistake," said Miss Greene.

Bath detectives are trying to find if there is any way the goods have escaped the binmen.

But a spokesman for Bath refuse disposal company, Pritchards, said there was little hope of finding the valuables if they had been collected in a plastic bag.

"It would have been compacted in the lorry and shredded with other refuse in Bath, then transferred by rail to Berkshire where it would be mixed with millions of tons of waste in a land-fill project," he said.

(from the *Bristol Evening Post*)

»»→

43

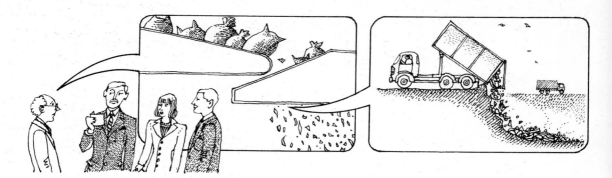

★ Use the list below to complete the table, putting together the words and phrases from the text that refer to the same thing.

ring   refuse disposal company
refuse   plastic bin liner
valuables   earrings
watch   waste
binmen

rubbish	dustmen
refuse	*refuse disposal company*
bag	mink coat and jewellery

jewellery

How to write a Chinese poem

詩

★ Read this with a dictionary (try not to look up more than ten words).

A well-known Japanese poet was asked how to compose a Chinese poem.

'The usual Chinese poem is four lines,' he explained. 'The first line contains the initial phrase; the second line, the continuation of that phrase; the third line turns from this subject and begins a new one; and the fourth line brings the first three lines together. A popular Japanese song illustrates this:

Two daughters of a silk merchant live in Kyoto,
The elder is twenty, the younger, eighteen.
A soldier may kill with his sword,
But these girls slay men with their eyes.'

(from *Zen Flesh, Zen Bones* compiled by Paul Reps)

A slice of bread

ALL BREAD starts from a simple recipe: you mix flour and water and cook it. Yet from this simple beginning come hundreds of different kinds of bread. There are flat breads from the Middle East and Asia and small thin sticks from Italy and southern Spain. The typical French loaf is long, thin, soft and white inside; German pumpernickel is dark and heavy and square. In many countries – Britain and Israel for example – you can find plaited loaves like the one in the picture.

Bread can be cooked in several ways: often it is baked in an oven, but chapattis (from India) and tortillas (from South America) are fried, and there's at least one bread that's boiled before it's baked. Bread can also include things other than flour, for instance onions, sausages, potatoes or fruit. One of the most unusual breads is lambrotsomo from Greece; this too is a plaited loaf and it's got whole eggs in the top – coloured red.

Croissants and sandwiches

When you think of the croissant you probably think of France, but according to one story they were first made in Hungary in 1686. The Turkish army was outside the walls of the city of Budapest. Early one morning the bakers of Budapest were making the day's bread when they heard something – it was the Turks making a tunnel through the city walls. The bakers woke the city up and Budapest was saved. To celebrate the occasion, the bakers made bread in the shape of the crescent moon on the Turkish flag – and croissants are still eaten today, hundreds of years after the battle and thousands of miles from Budapest.

⟫→

45

John Montague, fourth Earl of Sandwich (1718–92), is said to have invented the *sandwich* (which is certainly named after him) as the result of his passion for gambling. So reluctant was he to leave the gaming table – even for meals – that he ordered his waiter to bring him a cut of ham between two slices of bread, which he could eat without interruption of his play.

(from *A Dictionary of Eponyms* by C.L. Beeching)

Bread in your pocket, bread on the table

In countries where people eat a lot of bread words like 'bread' and 'dough' are sometimes used to talk about other important things. In English-speaking countries, for instance, 'bread' and 'dough' are both used to mean 'money'. Similarly, people talk about their jobs as their 'bread and butter', and the person in a family who brings home the money is called the 'breadwinner'. If you're very poor you might say that you're 'on the bread-line' – a memory of the days when poor people waited in a line to be given bread.

For many of us bread is something we eat so often that we don't think about it – until we go somewhere where the bread is different. If it's very different we may not even recognise it. The writer Colin Thubron heard this story from an old woman in Lebanon.

She knew how to bake mountain bread, slapping the dough between her forearms until she could spread it thinly. The villagers' ovens are curved iron plates, heated from below with sticks, and the bread is peeled off in huge circles, thin and mottled. When the French first came to Lebanon, she said, they found these pieces of bread neatly folded beside their plates, mistook them for table napkins, and tied them round their necks.

(from *The Hills of Adonis* by Colin Thubron)

Bread on the table, bread in the air

The most obvious thing to do with bread is to eat it. but there are other ways in which bread has been used. Here are three of them.

As a plate   In the past rich people used a large slice of bread as a plate. After the meal this was given to the poor to eat.

To remove marks   A small piece of bread can be used as a rubber to remove marks from art paper or wallpaper.

For air drops   Large objects can be dropped from an aeroplane using a parachute, but for smaller objects, like medicine or small tools, this isn't practical. After many experiments people interested in this problem decided that the answer was to put small things inside a loaf of bread. The reasons for this were:

1. You can get bread easily and cheaply almost anywhere.
2. The soft inside protects what you put in the loaf.
3. It's easy to see on grass and most other surfaces, so it's easy to find when it lands.
4. It's also easy to find on water, because it floats.

★ Look back at the text and find these words:

flour   loaf   bake   oven   slice   dough

Then put one word in each space under the pictures.

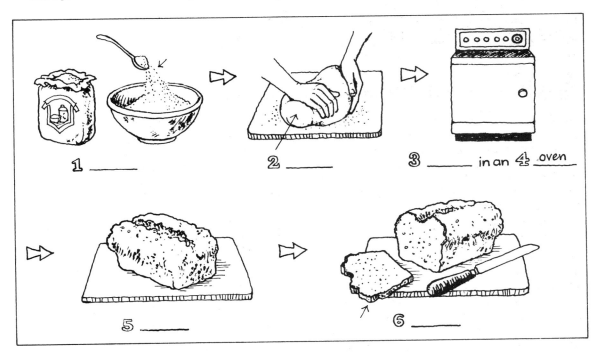

1 _____

2 _____

3 _____ in an 4 _____ oven

5 _____

6 _____

Eight lessons for robbers

IF YOU'RE fed up with your job, unemployed, or just short of money, why not rob a bank or a shop? All you need is a plan, a fast car, and perhaps one or two friends to help – and you'll never have to work or worry about money again. However, you can learn a lot from the mistakes of other robbers, so before you start some lessons may be useful.

1. **Remember – the idea is to have more money after the robbery, not less.** One man went into a shop thinking he had an easy way of getting a lot of money. He took out a £10 note and asked the shop assistant for change; when the assistant opened the till the robber took as much money as he could and ran out. Imagine his feelings when he discovered that he'd only got £5 from the till – and his £10 note was still in the shop.

2. **Before you disguise yourself – think.** One bank robber disguised himself very cleverly; he covered his teeth with silver paper. After the robbery the police couldn't get a description of him, because the silver teeth were the only thing people remembered.

   A mugger called Dean Saunders, however, didn't think enough about his disguise. After he committed a robbery, he dyed his red hair black. The police soon found him though – he was the only man in town with black hair and a red moustache.

3. **Choose a time when you'll get lots of money.** Some bank robbers in England in 1970 timed their robbery carefully. They planned to arrive when a large sum of money was leaving the bank. However, they arrived two minutes early – and instead of thousands of pounds, they got £250 each.

4. **Don't leave anything behind.** One robber wrote his note asking for money on notepaper with his name and address on it. Others have left behind clothes with names or addresses inside, wallets, and – when someone cut his hand trying to break into a travel agent's – part of a finger.

5. **Get away fast.** New York police arrested a man outside the shop he had just robbed. With his gun still in his hand, he had stopped to count the money.

6. **Use a car to make things easier, not more difficult.** Hoping to get away quickly, Joseph Durning left his car outside the bank with the engine running. However, the engine overheated, so when Joseph ran out of the bank and got into the car, it wouldn't move.

   Two students tried to rob a London bank, got nothing, and ran back to their car. When they got there, a policeman was waiting for them – because the car was badly parked.

   Another pair didn't do very well either – the driver couldn't find the robber. He was driving up and down the streets looking for his friend when two policemen asked him for a ride – they were looking for a robber . . . Soon afterwards, the robber found his driver – and two happy policemen.

7. **Choose a place where they speak your language.**

   A robber found Canada's language barriers too much when he went into a Vancouver bank for French-speaking residents and handed a cashier a note in English demanding money. The cashier, a recent immigrant from China, was unable to read it, and called a colleague for assistance.

   After puzzling over the note for several seconds the colleague asked the man to wait while he called the manager, who duly joined

in the fray. The man then mumbled something about 'money' in French, to which the bank manager replied: 'I'm sorry, but I don't speak English very well.'

In despair, the man asked for his note back, left the bank, and went into the English-speaking bank next door, where he started to go through the same procedure. This time he was more successful. The teller immediately handed over £500 in notes, and the raider, after thanking him in English, made off.

Don't become a robber if you're a kind person.

[A mugger*] pulled a gun on unemployed Salvatore Gioiello in a Naples street and ordered him to hand over all his cash.

He squirmed with embarrassment as Salvatore burst into tears and cried, 'If only I could. I've been out of work for two years and I have a wife and three children who are always hungry.'

Shamefaced, the crook took a well-filled wallet from his pocket and, pressing it into Salvatore's trembling hand, told him: 'Don't cry. Take this.' Then he turned and walked away.

Guessing the wallet, and the 100,000 lire (about £40) it contained had been stolen, Salvatore took it to the local police station.

*mugger: a robber who attacks people in the street

Three days later the owner called on Salvatore, gave him the 100,000 lire – 'For being so honest' – and promised to help him find a job.

The fate of the soft-hearted mugger is not recorded.

(from *The Book of Criminal Blunders* by Peter Mason and John Burns)

★ What happens when in the story about Salvatore? Put numbers 1 to 7 in the circles.

◯ The robber gave Salvatore the wallet.

◯ Salvatore started crying and explained his problems.

◯ The person who owned the wallet gave Salvatore the money.

◯ The robber felt terrible.

◯ The robber said to Salvatore, 'Give me your money.'

⑦ Nobody knows what happened to the robber.

◯ Salvatore gave the wallet to the police.

Good ideas

THESE days our lives are full of technological inventions – televisions, telephones, computers, microwave cookers and so on. But inventions like these don't solve all our problems, and sometimes they actually create new ones – like the Chernobyl disaster or people losing their jobs because of computers. Often they can't help us to solve the social problems that are all round us. That is why more and more people are becoming interested in a different kind of invention – the *social* invention.

What exactly is a social invention?

A social invention is any system or idea that can be used to solve social problems or improve people's lives. It may or may not use technology, but it won't be a piece of technology itself. A good example of a social invention is a baby-sitting circle, where a group of friends and neighbours arrange to baby-sit for one another. Instead of paying someone to look after their children when they go out, people in the circle 'earn' points by baby-sitting. They can 'spend' those points on a baby-sitter from the circle when they need one. The system uses no money and no technology. This is a small-scale social invention, but there are many large-scale ones in our world, for example schools and libraries.

Three social inventions

There are now several growing organisations round the world that are interested in the development of social inventions. The Institute for Social Inventions, based in London, is one of them. Every year the Institute has a competition with £1,000 in prizes, and the best ideas they receive are published in a book. To give an idea of just some of the things social inventors are thinking about, here are three inventions published by the Institute.

Zoo-Zoo vouchers

The owners of Zoo-Zoo, a natural foods restaurant in Oregon USA, decided to move to a larger place.

They borrowed as much money as they could from friends, but they still needed $10,000.

They raised this amount by pre-selling future meals, issuing $10 food vouchers, stamped 'Help the Zoo now' and with varied 'Valid after' dates – to prevent people redeeming them in one rush.

Even the carpenters working on the new premises accepted part payment in Zoo-Zoo food vouchers, and customers bought more than they would need to give to friends. Zoo-Zoo food voucher customers were their best advertisers, bringing friends who paid in dollars. Now with vouchers all redeemed, the restaurant is still flourishing, with 15 tables and 12 workers.

The Pet Fostering Service Scotland

Many older people who live alone keep pets for company. But what happens to an animal if its owner suddenly has to go away – to hospital for example? A social invention from Scotland has the answer.

►More than 350 volunteers throughout Scotland have offered their homes and foster care to animals in this situation. Social work departments and health boards have been advised of the service which is already widely used and appreciated. The only cost to the owner is for food. This is part of a policy to keep the owner in touch with the pet throughout the period of separation. Those who undertake the fostering service are encouraged to keep in touch with the owner either by letter or where possible by visiting, with or without the pet. [. . .]

Within the eighteen months since its inception, over 3,000 approaches have been made to the service – by community and hospital social workers, doctors, [. . .] relatives, etc. More than 200 pets have been fostered, some more than once; advice has been given and other arrangements have been made in over 100 cases, and many requests for help in walking a dog have been met. ◄

Eye signs on the road

Writer David Wade suggests that some people are in special danger when they cross the road. Children and tourists are the obvious examples but there are also the sufferers from 'ambiperplexity' – those people who find it difficult to remember which is left and which is right. Wade makes the following suggestion.

So as to reduce accidents among tourists, children and others when crossing streets, white eyes, with the pupils painted in indicating which way to look, would be painted on the road surface. [. . .]

Children, tourists and sufferers from 'ambiperplexity' all have their lives endangered, especially when crossing one-way streets, with traffic coming from an unexpected direction. 'Look left' or 'Look right' signs are not readily taken in, and the arrows sometimes used, although more direct, are ambiguous, because they can be taken to indicate the direction of traffic.

Wade suggests that eyes and pupils painted on the roads would save lives and would add to [. . .] the 'international pictogram language', found on road signs, cleaning labels and so on.

(from *Best Ideas, a Directory of Social Inventions*, edited by Nicholas Albery and Christine Mills)

★ Find these words and phrases between ► and ◄ and match them with their meanings.

policy	(help someone) to get news about
keep in touch with	beginning
period of separation	plan
undertake	(*a noun meaning*) asking
inception	agree to do something
request	when the old person has to be away from their pet

If you would like more information about the Institute for Social Inventions, write (including – for a reply – three International Reply Coupons, which you can get at a post office in your own country) to:

The Institute for Social Inventions
24 Abercorn Place
London
UNITED KINGDOM
NW8 9XP

Look what I've found!

A fisherman whose dog vanished as it swam across the Pechora river in northern Siberia later caught a 6ft-long pike, and noticed a tail sticking out of its jaws. He cut the fish open and the dog struggled out, barking, and none the worse for its experience, Moscow Radio claimed yesterday. – Reuter

(from *The Daily Telegraph*)

An Italian man has been caught on board a train in Dusseldorf carrying seven baby snakes hidden in socks, customs officials said yesterday. The man had wrapped up four anacondas, two boa constrictors and one poisonous coral snake in socks and then concealed them in his leather jacket. – Reuter

(from *The Guardian*)

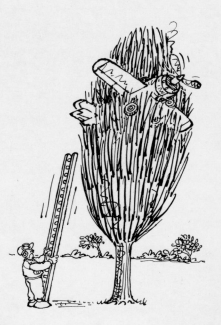

Thieves have stolen 2,249 manhole covers to sell back to Chinese government departments, bringing chaos to the streets of a north China city, especially for night time cyclists, an official newspaper said.

(from *The Western Daily Press*)

An aircraft that took off without its owner when he cranked its propeller to start it has been found, 65 miles away and up in the branches of a 35-ft poplar tree in Clifton, New York. – AP

(from *The Guardian*)

The bird man

NOT MANY people would like Eric Hosking's job. Part of the time he works outside – in all temperatures from boiling hot to freezing cold – and part of the time inside in the dark. When he's working he often has to sit still for hours. Sometimes he has to be a carpenter or an electrician, and he often has to carry heavy equipment to difficult and dangerous places. But to him it's all part of the job he loves – photographing birds.

Eric Hosking's long career has certainly had its moments of danger and excitement, but much of his time has been spent waiting quietly in a hide. Early photographers thought that a hide had to look like something that birds would recognise, so they built a 'cow' or a 'sheep' and stood inside it. The birds, it seems, didn't notice that the 'cow' had six legs. The kind of hide that Hosking usually uses, however, is rather like a small tent.

Early and modern hides

Four poles make the frame and two piece of material are placed over the top of the poles. The sides of the material are joined together but one side is left open as a door. The front of the hide has a hole about nine inches wide for the camera. To photograph birds nesting in trees a similar hide is built but with longer poles – sometimes as high as 60 feet above the ground.

Because birds often build their nests in places that are difficult for people to get to, hides sometimes have to be built in uncomfortable and dangerous places. If you want to photograph sea birds, for instance, you may have to build a hide high up on a cliff with only rocks and sea below. There can be other problems too – like the weather. Eric Hosking was once trying to get a picture of two hobbies during a thunderstorm. A pair of these rare and beautiful birds were using a nest near the top of a tall tree, so Hosking and some friends built a hide 64 feet above the ground to watch and photograph them.

One day Hosking saw both of the parent birds at the nest together – something nobody had ever photographed before. But a thunderstorm had begun, and the sky was too dark for a photo. All he could do was hope for a break in the storm before the birds left the nest, so with thunder and lightning all around he sat in the hide and waited. At last the sun came through the clouds for a few seconds – just long enough for him to take his photo.

⫸→

When he climbed down from the hide his hair was standing on end. Perhaps it was because of the electricity in the air; perhaps it was because he knew that at any time lightning could have struck the hide – which was higher than the trees and made of metal poles – and killed him instantly.

The 64 foot hide . . .   *. . . and the hobbies*

Taking photos from a hide is also hard work because the bird photographer has to sit still and wait for long periods of time. Most people find it hard to sit still for more than a few minutes; Eric Hosking often does this for eight or ten hours or more. On one occasion in Spain sitting still may have saved his life.

One afternoon while quiet and engrossed at the peep-hole, a Lataste's viper, the most poisonous snake in the area, slid into the hide, curled up between my boots and went to sleep. And there it stayed for four hours, fortunately undisturbed and therefore unaggressive. The slight noises and movements I made had no effect and it eventually slid out of the hide.

However, on another occasion Hosking didn't remain so calm, and – fortunately – he didn't wait in the hide either.

It was a pylon hide about 18 feet high, covered with hessian. Stuart Smith saw me settled in with my cameras, complicated flash gear and heavy batteries, and then left. It was a beautiful sunny day and the hessian was dry as tinder. Thinking a pipe would be pleasant, I lit up, dropped the match on the floor of the hide and stubbed it out with my boot – so I thought. But [. . .] before I knew what was happening the hessian was ablaze.

I poked my head out and yelled desperately to Stuart: 'I'm on fire!'

'Hope you fry!' he retorted, without turning round, obviously thinking I was joking.

I yelled even louder. 'Stuart!'

Recognising the urgency in my voice he rushed back, shouting: 'Your hair's on fire – bale out!'

(from *An Eye for a Bird* by Eric Hosking)

Somehow the two men got the cameras and equipment out of the hide; Hosking wasn't badly hurt, but the hide burnt to the ground.

★ Match these words from the story above with their meanings.

settled in   get very hot

light up   call loudly

ablaze   be funny

yell   burning, on fire

fry   come back quickly

joke   get out

rush back   light and begin smoking a cigarette, pipe etc.

bale out   organised and comfortable

Usually the bird photographer needs a helper for a simpler reason – he can't get into a hide without help from someone else. This is what happens. The photographer and a helper go to the hide, which is near the nest of the birds that are going to be photographed. When they go into the hide the birds fly away from the nest but watch it from a distance. The helper then leaves the hide and walks away. Since birds can't count, they don't know that there's still one person in the hide. They come to the nest and the photographer can take photos.

On one occasion, though, Hosking found that this didn't work. He was trying to photograph a pair of ravens at their nest, but the birds wouldn't come back to it. Then he remembered that ravens, according to some people, can count to four or five, so he got a class of local schoolchildren to walk to the hide with him. When the children walked away again the ravens soon came back to the nest, and he got his photos.

A raven . . . and its nest

⟫→

Eric Hosking has been photographing birds for 70 years or more. One of the surprising things about this is that early in his career he lost his left eye. He had been trying to photograph a tawny owl. One night as he was climbing up to his hide, the owl attacked him and damaged the eye, which later had to be removed in hospital. Twenty-four hours after leaving hospital he was taking photographs again – and a year later he got a picture of the same owl that had attacked him.

Not many people would like Eric Hosking's job, not many could do it – and probably no-one else in the world has taken so many beautiful photographs of birds.

The tawny owl that took
Hosking's left eye

A barn owl returns to the nest – Eric Hosking's most famous photograph

Last words

EVERYBODY has to die some day, but nobody likes to think about it. Even so, at some time in their lives most people manage to think about the question for long enough to make a will. If you've already made yours, it's probably just a few pages of writing leaving everything to your family. That's the kind of will that the majority of people make. However there are plenty of ways to make your will more interesting if you want to.

To begin with, you don't have to write it on paper. One man wrote his on an envelope, another on a door, and a third on an egg. It doesn't have to be a few pages either. You could copy Mrs Frederick Cook, who died in 1925; her will, longer than many novels, was more than 95,000 words long. If you haven't got time for that, however, you could take Herr Tausch as an example. His will, written in Czech in 1967, was just two words: 'Vše ženě' (All to wife).

For some people, the most important part of their will is the part that says how they want to be buried. Mrs Sandra West, a rich widow from Texas USA, decided that she wanted to be buried with her favourite things. When she died in 1977, her brother-in-law discovered that he would inherit $2.8 million – but only if he buried her in her favourite car. If he buried her any other way, he'd only get $10,000. It wasn't easy for Mrs West's brother-in-law, but two months after she died he got the permission he needed. Mrs West was buried in her blue Ferrari, and her brother-in-law became a rich man.

In 1973 dentist Philip Grundy from Leicestershire, England, left most of his money – £180,000 – to the nurse who worked for him. Lucky woman, you might think. There was a catch however; the money was hers after five years if in that time she didn't wear any kind of makeup or jewellery or go out with men. It is not known whether the nurse managed to wait for the five years to get the money.

Finally, let's hope that your will is not like that of Dr Everett Wagner, who lived in Kentucky USA 100 years ago. His family, who had not been to see him for years, suddenly began to visit him when he became ill; what was worse, each person suggested to Dr Wagner that they would like 'something to remember him by' when he died. Greatly annoyed with them, Dr Wagner wrote a will that would do this. To each of his four brothers he left one of his legs or arms; his nephew got his nose, and his two nieces each got an ear. His teeth and gums went to his cousins. He left $1,000 to pay for cutting up his body, and the rest of his money – $12,000, which was quite a large amount for those times – he left to the poor.

Answers

Shadow pictures

1 portrait   2 shadow   3 outline   4 fill in
5 frame   6 mount

Scallops

1897	Marcus Samuel Junior started the Shell Transport and Trading Company.
1971	The present Shell design was first used.
the 1840s	Marcus Samuel Senior started the family business buying shells in the Far East.
1904	Shell used a scallop shell design for their products for the first time.
1900	A mussel shell design was used for Shell products.

The sky is still blue

help you see again   2
see well   5
not see very much   1, 4
see nothing   3

Michelangelo, Martina and Marilyn

A

Iceland

Cold	Warm/Hot
icecaps	steam
glaciers	volcanoes
snow	lava
	greenhouses

What to do when someone's choking

casualty ——— hit
obstruction —— get (the food etc) out
slap ——— hand
dislodge ——— the choking person
remove ——— food etc in the windpipe
fist

Some other kind of people

they B	they B	they B
them O		
they O	they B	them O
They O	they O	
they O		
They B		
they B		
they O		

Is fashion as silly as it looks?

encourage ≠ undermine
dress ≃ wear
uniform ≠ freedom ≃ choice
fashion-conscious ≃ fashionable ≠ old-fashioned
silly ≠ sensible

Mum's snake

GOOD	BAD
rich	injured
full	lost
fortunate	difficulties
successful	thrilled

Dressing for the disco

By putting together the information in the first, second and last sentences you find there are 16 possible combinations of colours:

E– pink
A– mauve ——— B– scarlet
   C– mauve ——— D– pink (1)
   C– mauve ——— D– scarlet (2)
   C– scarlet ——— D– mauve (3)
   C– pink ——— D– mauve (4)

A– scarlet ——— B– mauve
   C– mauve ——— D– pink (5)
   C– mauve ——— D– scarlet (6)
   C– scarlet ——— D– mauve (7)
   C– pink ——— D– mauve (8)

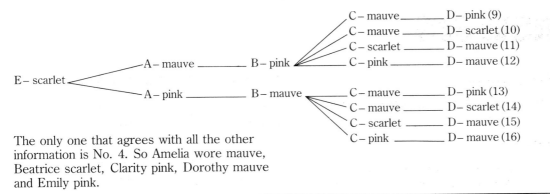

C – mauve _____ D – pink (9)
C – mauve _____ D – scarlet (10)
C – scarlet _____ D – mauve (11)
C – pink _____ D – mauve (12)

A – mauve _____ B – pink

E – scarlet

A – pink _____ B – mauve

C – mauve _____ D – pink (13)
C – mauve _____ D – scarlet (14)
C – scarlet _____ D – mauve (15)
C – pink _____ D – mauve (16)

The only one that agrees with all the other information is No. 4. So Amelia wore mauve, Beatrice scarlet, Clarity pink, Dorothy mauve and Emily pink.

Maui's fish

4 Maui's brothers tell him to stop, but he keeps pulling in his line.
6 Maui tells his brothers to wait till he comes back, but they don't.
1 Tired of his family's complaints, Maui decides to go fishing.
5 They find that Maui's fish-hook has caught land.
3 Maui's brothers catch lots and lots of fish – and then Maui starts fishing.
2 Maui makes his brothers go a long way out to sea.

Marion throws away £23,000

rubbish waste refuse	dustmen binmen refuse disposal company
bag plastic bin liner	mink coat and jewellery valuables
jewellery	
ring	watch	earrings

A slice of bread

1 flour   2 dough   3 bake   4 oven   5 loaf
6 slice

Eight lessons for robbers

4, 2, 6, 3, 1, 7, 5.

Good ideas

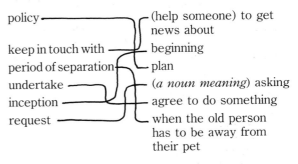

policy
keep in touch with
period of separation
undertake
inception
request

(help someone) to get news about
beginning
plan
(a noun meaning) asking
agree to do something
when the old person has to be away from their pet

The bird man

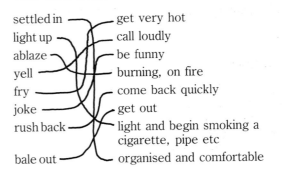

settled in
light up
ablaze
yell
fry
joke
rush back
bale out

get very hot
call loudly
be funny
burning, on fire
come back quickly
get out
light and begin smoking a cigarette, pipe etc
organised and comfortable

Acknowledgements

We would like to thank the following organisations, which have helped us in many different ways: Bridge International School of English, Bath; Cameron Balloons; the Institute for Social Inventions; NASA; The West of England Language Teachers' Association.

We are also grateful to all the friends, relations, colleagues and students who have helped and contributed in various ways, and in particular to Cathy Elston, Mike Moore and Brenda Proudfoot.

Something to Read 2 owes a great deal to the professional contributions of Alison Baxter and Peter Donovan of Cambridge University Press, and Kit Woods and Peter Ducker – to them our sincere thanks.

To Michael Swan and Catherine Walter our thanks for their continued support and advice.

The authors and publishers are grateful to the following for permission to reproduce photographs, illustrations and texts. It has not been possible to identify the sources of all the material used and in such cases the publishers would welcome information from copyright holders.

The Daily Mirror for the article on p. 2, and the adapted article and photograph on pp. 10–11; Paul Hamlyn Publishing for the adapted extracts from *Animal Oddities* by John May and Michael Marten on p. 3; Cambridge Animal and Public Health Limited for the photograph on p. 3; George Torres for the illustration from *Space Shuttle*, courtesy of Rockwell International on p. 5; Valerie Jackson for the extract from *Crafts*, Lutterworth Press on p. 6; the Victoria and Albert museum for the shilhouette on p. 6; Penguin Books Ltd for the extract from *Mediterranean Seafood* by Alan Davidson on p. 8, for the poem *Red and White* from *A Celtic Miscellany* by Kenneth Hurstone Jackson on p. 34 and the extract and poem from *Zen flesh, Zen bones* compiled by Paul Reps on p. 44, © Charles E. Tuttle Co. Inc; The Bridgeman Art Library for the reproduction of *The Birth of Venus* by Botticelli on p. 8; Thames and Hudson for the photograph on p. 8; Shell Education Service for the extract and drawings from *The Scallop* on p. 9; *The New Zealand Herald* for the adapted article and photograph on p. 11; Dr Miriam Stoppard for the extract from *The Baby Care Book*, Dorling Kindersley Ltd on p. 12; the Kobal Collection for the photographs (Charlie Chaplin, Robert de Niro, Marilyn Monroe) on p. 13; Colorsport for the photograph (Martina Navratilova) on p. 13; *Company* Magazine for the extract from an article on p. 13; Miles Kington for the adapted article from *The Independent* on p. 14; Don Philpott for the extract from *The Visitor's Guide to Iceland*, Moorland Publishing Co. Ltd on p. 16; David Williams for photographs from *Iceland, the Visitor's Guide*, Stacey International on pp. 15–17; J. M. Dent & Sons Ltd for the drawings and photograph from *Drawings* by Stephen Wiltshire on pp. 19–20; *The Daily Telegraph* for articles on pp. 21 and 52, © Reuters; *The Guardian* for articles on pp. 21 and 52, © Reuters and AP, and the photograph on p. 30; *The Western Daily Press* for articles on pp. 21 and 52; the *Western Mail* for the article on p. 21; All-Sport for photographs by Bob Martin on p. 23; Orbis Publishing for the extracts and drawings from *First Aid* by Ruth Thomson on pp. 24–5; Leonard de Vries for the drawings from *Victorian Inventions*, John Murray Ltd on pp. 25–7; Douglas Dickins Photo Library for the photograph of the Charles Russell painting (An American Indian hunting buffalo) and the Canadian High Commission for the engraving on p. 28; Faber and Faber for the adapted extracts from *Long Lance – the Autobiography of a Blackfoot Indian Chief* by Chief Buffalo Child Long Lance on p. 29; *The Observer Magazine* for the adapted extract and photogaph © Nick Briggs on p. 30; Cathy Elston for the drawing on p. 31; Stacey Knight for the photograph on p. 32; Sue Tatford for the photograph on p. 33 (top); photograph on p. 33 (bottom) © The Walt Disney Company; Weidenfeld & Nicolson Ltd for the poem *I through blue sky* from *Time for Lovers* by Robin Ray on p. 34; Albert Bonniers Förlag for the poem *Love me* by Maria Wine from *The Penguin Book of Women Poets* on p. 34; Penguin Books Australia for the adapted extracts and photographs from *A Fortunate Life* by Albert B. Facey on pp. 35–6; Methuen Publications (N.Z.) Ltd for the extract from *Diversions–Exercises for Mental Athletes* by F. P. Wilkins on p. 37; Guinness Publications Ltd for the adapted extract from *The Guinness Book of Records 1988* on p. 37; Antony Alpers for the adapted text and Patrick Hanly for the drawings from *Maori Myths and Tribal Legends*, John Murray on pp. 40–2; the *Bristol Evening Post* for the article on p. 4; Tony Stone Worldwide for the photograph on p. 45; C. L. Beeching for the extract from *A Dictionary of Eponyms*, Clive Bingley Ltd on p. 46; Colin Thubron for the extract from *The Hills of Adonis*, Penguin Books Ltd on p. 46; Peter Mason and John Burns for the adapted extracts from *The Book of Criminal Blunders*, Corgi on pp. 48–9; Institute of Social Inventions for the adapted extracts from *Best Ideas* edited by Nicholas Albery and Christine Mills on pp. 50–1; Eric Hosking and Frank W. Lane for the adapted extracts and photographs from *An Eye for a Bird*, Century Hutchinson Ltd on pp. 53–6.

Drawings by Shaun Williams pp. 1, 50, 51; Clyde Pearson pp. 6, 7, 12, 13, 24, 35, 36, 42, 53, 54; Tony Hall pp. 14, 48, 49, 57; Edward McLachlan pp. 21, 52; Chris Evans pp. 34, 37, 45, 47; Leslie Marshall pp. 38, 39, 43, 44; Peter Dennis p. 46. Maps by Reg Piggott Book designed by Peter Ducker MSTD